TWAYNE'S WORLD AUTHORS SERIES

A Survey of the World's Literature

CHINA

William R. Schultz, University of Arizona

EDITOR

Feng Chih

TWAS 515

Feng Chih

FENG CHIH

By DOMINIC CHEUNG

University of Southern California

TWAYNE PUBLISHERS
A DIVISION OF G. K. HALL & CO., BOSTON

Library of Congress Cataloging in Publication Data
Cheung, Dominic.
Feng Chih.

(Twayne's world authors series; TWAS 515 : China)
Bibliography: p. 113–19
Includes index.
1.   Feng, Chih, poet—Criticism and interpretation.
PL2760.E5Z62   895.1'1'5   78-14845
ISBN 0-8057-6356-2

To Feng Chih

Contents

About the Author

Dominic Cheung is Assistant Professor of Chinese and Comparative Literature at the University of Southern California. He finished his undergraduate studies at National Chengchi University in Taiwan, his Masters (English Literature) at Brigham Young University, and his Ph.D. (Comparative Literature) at the University of Washington, Seattle. He was associated with the International Writing Program at the University of Iowa in 1973–74, focusing his research on the Hundred Flowers Movement in Mainland China. A poet and critic as well as a scholar writing both in English and Chinese under the pen name of Ao Ao, his publications include *The Junior* (prose, 1965), *Transition* (poetry, 1966), *Death Antenna* (poetry, 1967), *Bird Cries* (poetry, 1971), *Contemporary American Poetry: A New Visage* (criticism, 1972), *From Mucha to Seattle* (prose & critical essays, 1976), *Selected Writings of Ao Ao* (1977), *Paterson* (a translation of William Carlos Williams' original work, 1978), and *Notes from the City of Lo* (poetry, 1978). His poetry has been anthologized in various volumes including *Poets of the Seventies, Poets of the Eighties,* and *Poetry in Sixty Years.*

Preface

In evaluating poems written over almost two-thirds of a poet's creative life, one should be able to assess the poet's creative output as a whole, with its fluctuating intensity, quality and direction, and select from it examples characteristic of his creativity. What criteria should we adopt to evaluate most appropriately the fluctuations of his creative activity? What should be our basis from which to determine the rise and fall of his creativity? In Feng Chih's case, the fluctuations were reflected in his experimentation with different modes of expression, resulting in the creation of new forms which uniquely accomodated the lyrical urge to the changing circumstances of each stage of his career. In this respect, his early lyrical poems, sonnets and narrative poems, as well as his later ballads, must all be viewed as crystallizations of his creative struggles.

I consider Feng Chih's life and art to be genuine reflections of the modern Chinese romantic movement, which manifested itself in various forms and guises in modern Chinese poetry. He is also, as Lu Hsun called him, "the most distinguished lyric poet in China." Together with the poetry of Ho Ch'i-fang and Pien Chih-lin, Feng Chih's sonnets and his other lyrics represent in modern Chinese poetry a unique lyricism which is the result of combining the European romantic concept of humanity and nature with traditional Chinese perspectives.

In the beginning of this book, I attempt to place Feng Chih in the context of his times, and to discuss the role he played in the lyric arena. I do so in order to view Feng Chih's poetic career in historical perspective, providing an important introduction to our assessment of his poetry as the epitome of modern Chinese lyricism. In a rather confusing but nevertheless exciting milieu where experimentation always took command in literary matters, Feng Chih's slow, contemplative revelation of his feelings found its most appropriate expression in the sonnet form, in which he was able to avoid the deluge of sentimentalism which so often characterizes the works of his contemporaries. His sonnets are distinguished among the new forms of his time, both in their craftmanship and in their philosophic content.

Feng Chih's poetic creation moved from an individualistic overflow of subjective emotions in his early years to a mass-oriented singing of ballads in his later years. Within this overall shift in direction in the development of his creative activities, I regard the sonnets as the point of maturation, and his lyric-narratives as part of that process of maturation. If I am wrong in choosing the sonnets as the finest expression of his genius, Feng Chih would still be in his lyric ascent. Throughout my treatment of Feng Chih's poetry, I have maintained that the lyric poet should write as a subjective self rather than as an objective viewer. His songs should flow from the nurturing of his inner mind and not reflect the outer demand of an ideology. The fact is that since 1949 Feng Chih's efforts to write for external causes obviously created a dilemma for the lyrical poet whose subjective self stood central to his imaginative endeavor, a dilemma which has contributed to the ebb of his lyricism.

Yet there are some other factors we should consider as well. Since 1949, socialist literature has been the dominant trend in China, in which a writer's purpose is not to find pleasure for himself but to labor for the masses. Singing alone is not important, and is even considered parasitic. To sing for the relief of the people and learn from the people, for the betterment of the people's struggle for socialism, is now the main task of the Chinese poet. Feng Chih has carefully and faithfully followed these social and political developments, and this has resulted in his efforts to write in the balladic mode. Although his later work clearly indicates departure from his earlier lyrical writings, his experiments with the ballad form mark only another of his efforts to achieve a breakthrough in his longstanding search for a form which will accomodate his experience. The ballad form can even be regarded as a possible extension of his narrative poetry.

This new turn, that is, the writing of the new ballads, reflects the poet's serious intention to accomodate himself to the needs of society and to the new demands made on poets. Unlike Ai Ch'ing, who chose to remain faithful to his past convictions, Feng Chih has tried to move with events, adjusting himself steadily to changing times. From this perspective, shall we say Feng Chih's creativity is still in its ascendancy? Or is it about to make a new ascent? I believe that Feng Chih has tried to achieve another breakthrough, the results of which may best be evaluated in terms of his new endeavor to write for the masses, not in terms of the criteria which he had set for himself in the past as a subjective lyrical poet, and which he claims to have abandoned in his new phase of creative activity.

My research on Feng Chih started when I studied with Professor Hellmut Wilhelm, a good friend of Feng Chih who possesses a great deal of firsthand information on his early poetic career. I also learned much from Professor Vincent Shih's enlightened talks and writings on the modern Chinese literary scene. The time and help given me by Professors C. H. Wang, David Knechtges and the late Arthur Oberg in completing a dissertation on Feng Chih at the University of Washington is much appreciated.

Both the form and content of this book have undergone substantial changes from the original version. During a period of residence at the University of Iowa I was able to study the recent verse of Feng Chih. Professors Paul and Hua–ling Nieh Engle arranged a year of postdoctoral research for me in the International Writing Program at the University of Iowa, and their kindness and assistance are deeply appreciated. I am particularly indebted to Professor Noriko Mizuta Lippit, colleague and dear friend of mine at the University of Southern California, for reading my manuscripts with great patience and understanding. Her comments and suggestions enriched my own approach to Feng Chih's splendid lyricism, and she also helped immeasurably in the writing process. Professor Laurence Thompson, also of the University of Southern California, and my editor, Professor William Schultz of the University of Arizona, have been most generous and enthusiastic in helping me ready this book for print. Professor William Tay of the Chinese University of Hong Kong helps me tremendously in updating Feng Chih's current events. I wish to thank Ms. Patricia Blinde and Ms. Janice Bender for their help with the English, and Ms. Cassandra Kao for her assistance with the notes and bibliography. Acknowledgment should also go to the University of Southern California Summer Research and Publication Fund for making possible the completion of this manuscript. And last, but not least, I thank my wife and daughter—source of my stability and encouragement all these years.

Dominic Cheung (Ao Ao)

University of Southern California

Chronology

1906   Born in Cho-hsien, Hopei.

1920   Graduated from high school.

1923   Matriculated at Peking University; wrote "Returning Home."

1925   Editor of *Ch'en-chung* (*The Sunken Bell*).

1927   *Tso-jih chih ko* (*Songs of Yesterday*) published; trip to Harbin.

1928   "Northern Journey" published; graduated from Peking University.

1930   Left for Germany to study at the University of Berlin.

1931   *Briefe an einen jungen Dichter* (*Kei i-ko ch'ing-nien shih-jn ti shih-feng-hsin*) translated.

1935   Doctorate received from the University of Berlin; returned to China.

1937   Essay on Goethe's *West-östlicher Divan* published in *Wen-hsüh tsa-chih*.

1938   Sino-Japanese War; went to Kunming, made professor of Southwest Associated University.

1939–   The sonnets composed.
1940

1941   Concentrated on the study of the Chinese classics, focusing on authors such as Tu Fu and Lu Yu.

1942   *Shih-ssu-hang chi* (*The Sonnets*) published.

1946   *Wu Tzu-hsü* published.

1947   *Shan Shui* (*Landscape*) published.

1949   *The Sonnets*, second edition.

1950   February made member, Second National Committee, All-China Federation of Literature and Art Circles, and administrative committee member, Chinese Writers' Association; February 1950 sent to tour Eastern European Communist countries; after return to China published *Tung-ou tsa chi* (*Miscellaneous Notes on East Europe*).

1952   *Tu Fu Chuan* (*The Life of Tu Fu*) published; made director, Research Institute of Foreign Languages and Literature until present. December made member of delegation to attend World Peace Congress in Vienna.

1953 *Tu Fu Chuan*, second edition; trip to Soviet Russia.

1954 *Tu Fu Chuan*, third edition; January made professor of Peking University; August elected deputy for Honan to first National Peoples' Congress.

1955 *Feng Chihh shih-wen hsüan-chi (Selected Poems and Prose)* published; made member, Foreign Literature Committee, Chinese Writers' Association; June made member, Department of Philosophy and Social Sciences, Chinese Academy of Sciences.

1956 *Hai-nieh shih hsüan (Poetry of Heine)* published.

1958 July, made member, Chinese People's Committee for Defense of World Peace.

1959 *Shih-nien shih ch'ao (Poems of Ten Years)* published.

1960 August, made member, Third National Committee, All-China Federation of Literature and Art Circles.

1963 *Shih yu i-ch'an (Poetry and Its Legacy)* published; December, led delegation of Chinese writers to visit Cuba.

1964 "Memoir in Cuba," fifteen classical poems published in *Shih-k'an (Poetry)*.

1977 After a long period of silence, Feng's poems and reviews began to re-appear in *Shih-kan* following the purge of the "gang of four."

1978 Heine's *Deutschland, Ein Wintermarchen* translated and published; essay on "Chinese adaptation of Western materials" *(Lun yang wei chung yung)* appeared in *Ta-kung pao*.

CHAPTER 1

Feng Chih and His Times

FENG Chih's life and times can be divided into three periods which coincide with three prominent stages of modern Chinese history: the prewar period (1921–1932), the war period (1932–1946), and, finally, the postwar period (1946–present). The year 1921 is an appropriate date to start with because in that year Feng Chih, then fifteen years old, left his home town of Cho-hsien, a small rural community in Hopei province, and went to study in Peking. It was also the time of the great forward movement in Chinese literature, with writers following the lead of Ch'en Tu-hsiu (1879–1942) and Hu Shih (1891–1962), both of whom, writing in the journal *New Youth*, advocated the democratization of literature by writing in vernacular Chinese. Most important of all, 1921 was the year in which the Literary Research Association, the first literary group of the post-May Fourth era, was established.

Although China had not been without a tradition of literary groups or factions in the past, the forming of the Literary Research Association was unique because it represented a literary viewpoint, different from that of the past or contemporary times, which stressed "art for life's sake" in order to restore high seriousness to literature. The Association was first organized in January, 1921, with a Manifesto and a set of Abridged Regulations.[1] The Manifesto stated three principles: 1) to collect and disseminate information on literature and to reconcile differences between classical and modern studies; 2) to introduce new techniques and knowledge; and 3) to regard literature as a work of life, comparable to that of workers and peasants, and to discard playful attitudes towards the creation of literature. The strictness of these principles would suggest a highly disciplined literary movement, but the Association eventually proved to be no more than a gathering of writers who wished to take life and literature seriously. According to Mao Tun (1896–   ), one

15

of the leading figures in the Association, the ideas of the group could be likened to a pan of scattered sand rather than a coherent ideology capable of determining the literary directions of the time.[2] There was neither an "attempt" nor a "desire" by the members of the Association to achieve a common set of principles. If there had, it would only have been a declaration that the time to view literature as a playful object, a pleasant pastime, was past.

Another literary group, the Creation Society, was formed in the same year by a group of writers educated in Japan, and headed by such literary figures as Yu Ta-fu (1896–1945), Kuo Mo-jo (1892–1978) and Ch'eng Fang-wu (1894–   ). The emergence of the Creation group represented an antithesis to the ideal of realism promulgated by the Literary Research Association writers. It should be noted that Mao Tun, for one, insisted strongly that since there had never been a consensus among the Association writers to set up a literary principle of art for life's sake, there were no clique activities to reflect it as a basic attitude.[3]

Nevertheless, viewing the reaction of the Creation writers to the Literary Research Association group, it is obvious that the Creation group adopted a more artistic sensibility and sought to employ the more imaginative practice of romanticism. Ch'eng Fang-wu, the critic of the group, viewed realism in terms of genuine realism and pseudo-realism, labelling the latter "Trivialism," a term taken from M. Guyau's *L'art Au Point De Vue Sociologique*.[4] Ch'eng stated that realistic literature is an awakening of the romantic dream and a return to the self, an attempt to face reality directly in its ultimate dimensions. However, in observing reality, "we must catch its inner life, rather then be infatuated by its outer phenomena. We must present the entirety of life in our expressions, making the partial descriptions connote the whole, or making it relate to and exist as part of the whole . . . . Trivial writers see only superficial colors and partial outlooks; they are merely making photographs and records."[5]

Ch'eng argued that the romanticism of the Creation group was not an escape from life, but a reflection, a resistence, and a protest against the reality of life in China. Another writer, Cheng Po-ch'i (1895–   ) recognized three sources of their romanticism. First, the Creation writers who studied overseas, mostly in Japan, had experienced a double frustration. They had seen the weakness of capitalism, and at the same time, the sickness of semicolonial China. Second, the nostalgia created by their prolonged sojourns overseas was followed by an enormous feeling of emptiness after their return, a feeling compounded by the various frustrations they encountered in their own country. When they were overseas, they were pensive and nostalgic, but after they returned, they were agitated and emotional. Third, Western ideas had influenced them greatly during the time they were abroad, especially the rejection both of rationalism in philosophy and naturalism in literature. This is why they all found inspiration in an antirational romanticism.[6]

Apart from the practices of the Literary Research Association and the Creation Society writers, the concept of formalism in poetry brought in by the Crescent Society greatly influenced the young poets such as Feng Chih and Ho Ch'i-fang (1910–77). The Crescent Society was formed by Wen I-to (1899–1946), Hsu Chih-mo (1896–1931) and several others, who all began to write for the *Peking Morning Post Supplement* in 1926, when Feng Chih was twenty. Two years later, the *Crescent Monthly* was published by this same group of people, who emphasized the need to discover new poetic forms and rhythms. Wen I-to, who sought to perfect new metrical patterns in modern Chinese poetry, must have been a major influence on Feng Chih's commitment to find new regulated forms for his poems. Feng's adoption of the Western sonnet form was undoutedly a product of this influence. However, it should be noted that although the emphasis on form favored by the Crescent poets affected Feng greatly, the sometimes muted lyricism of most Crescent poets never deterred Feng Chih from giving voice to his own social sensibilities. Most of his poems written at that time show a depth of social committment, a concern for the social and political environment and for the masses, rather than an intoxication with his own individual emotions.

The establishment of the *Sunken Bell* in 1925, a literary journal whose name was adopted from Gerhart Hauptmann's play *Die Versunkene Glocke*, marked the closing phase of Feng Chih's first poetic stage. Only a year before, in 1924, Feng had joined the literary group associated with the *Shallow Grass Quarterly* in Shanghai, a journal which sought to promote the aesthetic ideas of truth and beauty. According to Lu Hsun (1881–1936), these writers were making an effort "to absorb foreign nutrients externally and to explore the individual soul internally, an attempt to discover the inner vision to gaze at the universe and the inner voice to sing to the lonely people with truth and beauty."[7] Nevertheless, Lu Hsun subsequently came to abhor the pessimistic attitudes expressed by these writers and to condemn their foreign borrowings as no more than the essence of *fin de siècle* attitudes borrowed from Wilde, Nietzsche, Baudelaire and Andreyev. The termination of the *Shallow Grass Quarterly* the next year, and the relocation of part of the editorial staff from Shanghai to Peking, where they later established the *Sunken Bell*, enabled Feng Chih to edit his new journal in the more serious manner he desired. Evaluating the *Sunken Bell*, Lu Hsun's praise was highly laudatory. He viewed the struggles of the journal as being the "most elastic, sincere, and endurable in China."[8] The *Sunken Bell* writers were "laboring to their deaths like bell-casting workers, who tolled with their feet after the bell was sunken."[9] However, Lu Hsun regretted that the Chinese reading public was too numb and sterile to appreciate their efforts.

Poorly received by the public, the *Sunken Bell* folded following its eighth year of publication. It had begun in October, 1925, as a rather ambitious literary weekly in Peking. The following year, after only four issues had been published, it was changed to a bimonthly publication. Financial pressures were probably the prime motive for this change, but it also allowed the editors more time to prepare copy which introduced its Chinese readership to modern German literature. Twelve issues of the bimonthly appeared prior to the cessation of publication in the autumn of 1927. The journal was revived five years later, in the autumn of 1932, and twelve consecutive issues were again published on a bimonthly basis. Feng Chih's first collection of poetry, *Songs of Yesterday,* was published in 1927 as one of four *Sunken Bell Literary Books* printed by the Pei-hsin Bookstore in Peking.

How was the Sunken Bell Society formed? Ch'en Hsiang-ho, an initiator of the group, refused to admit that *Sunken Bell* was a metamorphosis of *Shallow Grass*.[10] Although all the *Sunken Bell* editors wrote for *Shallow Grass*, they do not seem to have known each other directly until *Shallow Grass* folded. It was not until early autumn in 1925 that these writers gathered in Peking and decided to form a literary society. The name *Sunken Bell* reflected not only the title of Hauptmann's play, but also the autumn season, when the sounds of cicadas were loudly heard. In addition, the bleakness of the early autumn sky in northern China conveyed a strong sense of isolation.[11] The journal was first published and wholesaled by the Pei-hsin Bookstore, but the wholesale rights to the journal were later rescinded because of the inefficient operation of the bookstore. Feng Chih proofread and helped to mail out the journal. His own *Northern Journey* was published in 1929 and again listed as one of the *Sunken Bell Literary Books*. Although sales were unsatisfactory, Feng Chih came to establish himself as a leading lyricist, particularly with his long narrative poems.

Feng left China for Germany in 1930 and did not return until 1935. During his absence, China as a nation suffered heavily under foreign exploitation. The foreign concessions in Shanghai, then China's main cultural center, and imperialistic pressures from the foreign powers caused most Chinese writers to become conscious of their semicolonial status. In 1932, the Chinese Poetry Society was organized in Shanghai with the following statement; "In semi-colonial China, we live under a heavy thunderstorm. Many poetic materials are to be absorbed and to be expressed by us, but, unfortunately, our poetry arena is silent. Most poets are westernized and intoxicated with romantic flowers and moonlight . . . . Writing poetry apart from the people is inappropriate in this great time."[12] The literary direction of the Society, therefore, was not to view poetry as visual art, but to emphasize its practical function as a political weapon, so that it would be united with the masses, not with the chosen audience of the poet. Poems written by such members of the Society as Mu Mu-t'ien (1900–) are more prosaic, colloquial and usually of longer length than the lyrics of their contemporaries, who tended to labor the poet's individual passion. Their political stance was clear—to fight against imperialism and to expel the Japanese invaders. Their slogan of "Defense Poetry" was the prototype for the slogan "Defense Literature" which was widely adopted during and after the war.

With the outbreak of the Sino-Japanese War, poets began to write as war poets rather than as pure lyricists. Ai Ch'ing (1910–), T'ien Chien (1914–) and Tsang K'o-chia (1910?–) were among those who sang of the battlefield. Although there was no formal grouping of these poets into societies, they became more united than ever. Among them, Hu Feng (1904–), who did not really excel as a poet, contributed greatly in leading modern Chinese poetry to a more revolutionary level as an editor of two journals, *July* and *Hope*, during and after the war.

When Feng Chih returned to China in 1935, he first joined the faculty of the German department at Peking University and was mostly concerned in his academic efforts with introducing German literature to China. These efforts were mainly in the form of translations and commentaries, such as Feng did with Nietzsche's poems. After the war broke out, Feng retreated with other scholars to southwest China where he taught at the renowned Southwest Associated University at Kunming, where many writers and scholars had gathered to teach. Feng remained in Kunming throughout the war from 1938 to 1946.

His writings during these years were mostly concerned not with major national events, but with the small, common matters of daily life. He possessed the philosophic temperament to convert trifling things into meaningful ones, and to transform agitated feelings into tranquil moods. Like Pien Chih-lin (1910–   ), Feng Chih was a lyricist who insisted on tackling reality in his own lyrical terms, and this succeeded in heightening the lyric tension in his poems. However, that poetry lacked the common passion which could appeal to the masses, particularly during the war years, when many poets were taking an active role in communicating with the people and advocating that they join in the struggle to expel the Japanese invaders. His lyrical poems were the product of intellectuals conversing with intellectuals, and they often require very sophisticated interpretation. Feng's *The Sonnets* is a typical example of this kind of success and failure.

Sha Ou's article on the "Exile of Lyricism" conveys the feeling and message of a lyric poet writing in those days. He says:

Maybe on the road to exile, you are amazed to see the scenic landscapes you have not come across before. And yet, the vigor and magnificence of scale and degree of this war have repeatedly strangled our interest in being lyrical. Although one may feel that the landscapes are so rich in their lyrical fragrance, yet they seem to be so ridiculous. People died from bombing. Lyricism died from bombing. What was left is poetry, and her responsibility is to describe our spirit which refuses to die from bombing.[13]

While Feng Chih was still in Kunming, the questions of "National Forms" and the merging of the writer's art with the consciousness of the masses, much discussed in Yenan, became one of the central issues of modern Chinese literature. In 1938, Mao Tse-tung proclaimed in his famous article "The Position of the Chinese Communists in the National War" that the great force of Marxism-Leninism was to merge with the revolutionary practices of each individual nation. Chinese communists had to learn how to practice

Marxism-Leninism in their own Chinese context, and to unite the contents of internationalism with national forms, namely, common expressions from the common people. Therefore, "all foreign eight-legged practices have to be discarded; hollow, abstract tunes have to be sung less; dogmatism has to retire. What takes over will be the vivid, resilient Chinese style and character, which the masses are happy to see and hear."[14] Mao was thereby trying to make his followers conscious of their own national origins, so that they could adopt foreign political theories and digest them in their own context, without changing completely the whole cultural basis of the nation. In literary terms, the implication of Mao's statement is that although it is inevitable for writers to absorb foreign ideas and experiences, they have to express themselves in a way the masses understand and appreciate—foreign conservativism ("eight-legged practices"), nihilism and dogmatism are to be avoided. Most important of all is that literature must serve the masses; it must be "non-foreign" so that the masses will respond to it happily.

The two leading journals in Yenan, *Battle Line of Literature and Art* and *Chinese Culture*, immediately responded to Mao's ideas on national forms with open discussion. Later on, the discussions spread to Chungking in the Kuomintang area where Hu Feng was staying. Two publications, the *Hsinhua Daily* and the *Literature Monthly* had organized separate sessions to discuss the issue. In Chungking, the issue of national forms became a cause of controversy.

First, Hsiang Lin-ping dissociated "artistic forms" from "popular forms." In a series of articles ("On National Form and Its Main Source," "The Use of Popular Forms and the Creation of National Forms," and "A Second Article on National Form and Its Main Source"), Hsiang contended that popular forms are literary types commonly used by the masses and therefore they should be adopted as the appropriate means of literary expression. On the other hand, artistic forms are only "abnormally developed city products," which are used by "university professors, bankers, ballroom dancers, politicians and petty bourgeoise."[15] These artistic types are only by-products of the May Fourth influence, and lack the essential colloquial elements which are always present in popular forms. Therefore, they must be placed in a secondary position in the creation of national forms, or a new national literature.

Hsiang's articles immediately provoked a defense of the May Fourth era literature. If Hsiang's contentions were valid, it was argued, then the innovations of the May Fourth Movement in founding a new literary idiom and sensibility would be erased. And certainly, the mainstream of the May Fourth writers consisted of more than just university professors or ballroom dancers, although it is true that some treaty port writers did write and talk like bar-girls. Among its defenders, Ho Ch'i-fang, Kuo Mo-jo, Chou Yang (1908–) and Hu Feng pointed out that it was essential for the May Fourth literature movement to merge with a national cultural revolution. There was a tie between the classical and modern literature in which the new developed out of, but was not totally detached from, the old. Old and new forms should not be antagonistic to each other; old popular forms adopted by the common people could not negate the significance of the new artistic forms developed by the new writers.[16]

Mao Tse-tung's subsequent discussion on literature and art at the Yenan Forum in 1942 brought the consideration of national forms to a higher level of interpretation. The search for national forms was a search for appropriate models, Chinese in origin, to serve the workers, peasants and soldiers. There were writers who came to Yenan from Kuomintang areas and their non-Marxist view of literature resulted in a narrowness of view and expression, which, it was claimed, was contradictory to the popular usages of the masses. Their mistakes, according to Mao, had contributed to the common practices of idealism, dogmatism, utopianism, empty talk, contempt of practice and aloofness from the masses.[17] Although there was a question of whether popularization or elevation should come first, Mao made it clear that "every class in every class society places the political criterion first and the artistic criterion second," and we have to be aware of the fact that "some things which are basically reactionary from the political point of view may yet be artistically good. But the more artistic such a work may be, the greater the harm it will do to the people, and the more reason for us to reject it. The contradiction between reactionary political content and artistic form is a common characteristic of literature and art of all exploiting classes in their decline. What we demand is unity of politics and art, of content and form, and of the revolutionary political content and the highest possible degree of perfection in artistic form."[18] Here, Mao made clear that regarding popularization and elevation, the former was to take precedence over the latter.

The discussion of "National Forms" and Mao's "Talks at the Yenan

Forum on Literature and Art" had a great impact on Feng Chih's creative activities after the Liberation. As we know, Feng himself emerged as an artistic product of the May Fourth literature movement, and together with other poet-scholars, he worked consciously towards the perfection of form as a means of expressing his artistic sensibilities.

With the Liberation, Feng seems to have changed his literary views completely. First, he insisted in one of his later poetry collections that he, together with his poetry, had experienced a rebirth after the birth of the People's Republic of China.[19] In other critical essays, he refers constantly to the discussions of national forms in 1938 and, like all writers in the People's Republic of China, the literary directions set forth by Mao in the Yenan Talks. In an article called "Problems of Form in New Poetry," which first appeared in *Criticism on Literature and Art* in 1959 and was later collected in his book *Poetry And Legacy,* published in 1963, Feng addresses the question of form, particularly the dilemma concerning new poetic forms to communicate with the masses. He refers to Mao's idea that national forms should be one with Chinese style and character, and to the liking of the masses. In addition, Stalin's famous saying "Proletarian content and national form" is adopted to reveal Feng's full awareness of the necessity of political content in poetry. He says, "Content is vital and decisive. What is primary is the political implication."[20] In discussing the relationship between form and content, he continues, "To talk of form without content will only lead to the blunder of being a formalist; but if the problem of content is settled and that of form is overlooked, we are still wrong because the problem of form in new poetry is not to be solved in terms of content alone."[21] Feng insisted that political content is vital.

Regarding form, it is necessary to discover traditional Chinese forms, and especially those that are popular among the people. According to Feng, there are two ways of finding a national form. One is to learn from traditional classical poetry, to study the economy of language and the musical and imagistic significances which distinguished the verse of poets of the past. The other way is to learn from the new ballads created by the masses directly from their labor experiences. Since these ballads have a genuine political content and exist as a popular form among the common people, new poets should express their ideas in the balladic form in order to achieve a true reflection of reality. Feng Chih's latest collection of poems, *Poetry In Ten Years*, is an example of this purpose and endeavor.

To conclude, Feng Chih's poetic career reflects the entire development of modern Chinese poetry, with the three stages in his career corresponding to major points of transition in modern Chinese literature. The primary stage of growth consisted of breaking away from the bondage of traditional forms and language. The secondary stage was one of absorption, of integrating foreign forms and styles in order to perfect form and content. The final stage was one of momentous change, of the pursuit of a union between the poet, the masses, and socialist ideology. Feng Chih's late years mark the beginnings of a new era of socialist realism in China; and his synthesis of past experience and present understanding bears witness to a bright future for modern Chinese poetry.

CHAPTER 2

The Role Feng Chih Played in the Lyric Arena

O F the work of the many new poets who produced hybrids of East-West verse in the 1930s, that of Feng Chih stands out as a distinctive contribution to the development of modern Chinese poetry. Lu Hsun called him "the most distinguished lyric poet of China,"[1] and Chu Kuang-ch'ien, in assessing Feng's role, saw him as a poet who successfully integrated the emotional and the rational in his compositions.[2] The results of this careful balance, Chu noted, were the distinctive poetic images which are uniquely Feng's. Among Feng's contemporaries, the members of the Crescent school, which included the poets Hsu Chih-mo and Wen I-to, produced works which were, in Chu Kuang-ch'ien's estimation, immature in both form and choice of subject. Likewise, those, like Pien Chih-lin and Mu Tan, who chose to write after the school of the French Symbolists and Anglo-American modernists, were often obscure and narrow in their poetic practices.[3]

In seeking a balance between reason and emotion, Feng aligned himself with the German modernists. In this, Feng was unique among his contemporaries. Even Tsang K'e-chia who, Chu Kuang-ch'ien notes, "followed the unadorned, direct expression of the ballads in his early days," failed to maintain a balance between the emotional and the rational in his later works.[4] According to Chu's evaluation, despite diverse influences from the West, few Chinese poets successfully managed to integrate Western poetic practices with Chinese subjectivity and produce poetry of sustained excellence.

In spite of the essentially bleak view which emerges from Chu Kuang-ch'ien's evaluation of the literary scene of pre-World War II China, Feng's poetic achievement and his successful integration of feelings and reason in terms of the Chinese notion of "passions

25

dissolving into reason" (*yung ch'ing yu li*) can perhaps best be appreciated in relation to the works of his contemporaries. In assessing the emotional tenor of the poetry composed in Feng's day and the distaste he felt for the sentimentality which pervaded the works of his compatriots, it is perhaps appropriate that we examine Hsu Chih-mo's poem, "This is a World of Cowardice." This poem has all the features which characterize Feng's own definition of the "lifeless lyric."

> This is a world of cowardice,
> Without love, without love!
> Untie your hair,
> Let your feet go bare;
> Follow me, my love,
> Forsake this world,
> Sacrifice our love!
>
> I am holding your hand,
> Love, you follow me:
>   Let thorns pierce through our soles,
>   Let hail crack our heads,
> I am holding your hand,
>   Fleeing from the cage, regain our freedom!
>
> Follow me,
> My love!
> The human world is already behind us.
> Look! Isn't this a large clouded sea?
> A large clouded sea,
> A large clouded sea,
>   A boundless freedom, for you and me and love!
>
> Follow my index finger and look,
> A tiny azure point at the end of the sky—
>   That is an island, green grass on it,
>   And flowers, beautiful beasts and fowls;
> Hurry to this swift boat,
> Depart for that ideal paradise—
> Love, joy, and freedom—away from the human world forever![5]

Evident in Hsu's poem are strains of English romanticism as well as borrowings from the Victorian period. In its search for a better world, Hsu's work thematically echoes both Tennyson's "Locksley Hall" and Shelly's "Hellas." The effect created by the poem's verbosity and melodramatic tone, however, is stilted and fails to accomplish the poem's purpose of evoking an ardent desire to create a utopian existence. If, as Chu noted, emotions cannot sustain a poem, it is even more apparent that the simulated intensity of emotions artfully cloaked in flamboyant rhetoric, the quality which characterizes Feng's "lifeless lyric," cannot possibly rise to the level of true poetry.

In contrast to Hsu's easy magniloquence, Feng Chih's own work "I Can Only Sing" is a poet's painful realization that art is finally a poor rendition of life itself.

> I can only sing . . .
> Sing of this musical dusk:
> It is gossamer flying in the air,
> Duckweed floating on the water,
> A leaf falling in the wind,
> The drifting of flower tassels,
> Flimsy, loveless,
> Flimsy, loveless!
>
> I can only sing . . .
> Play this music in the middle of the night,
> The player of the lute is the chill wind outside
>   the window,
> The solo, the weak pumping of my heart,
> No audience
>   Save for my own spirit,
> Dead, loveless,
> Dead, loveless!
>
> How can I write
> the great song of high noon
> that has red flowers, green leaves, bright sun,
> hope, despair, fantasy,
> graves, wedding feasts,
> births, deaths?
> Joyfully, all but love.
> Joyfully, all but love![6]

A poet's creation, Feng Chih implies, is a "musical dusk" and the vagueness with which true life experiences are conveyed in poetry are as " . . . gossamer flying in the air" and as ephemeral as "duckweed floating on the water,/ A leaf falling in the wind." The task of approaching the intensity and magnitude of life which Feng sees as "the great song of high noon," seemingly lies beyond human capacities, for the poet asks "How can I write [such a song,]" with its " . . . red flowers, green leaves, bright sun,/ Hope, despair, fantasy,/ graves, wedding feasts,/ births [and] deaths."

While Feng's intellectual recognition of the enormity of human emotions and life experiences sets him apart from his fellow poets, who simply plunged into the task of venting personal sentiments, nevertheless, in his own early works he was not above giving voice to sentimental inclinations of his own. In his well known narrative "Northern Expedition," for instance, we read:

> The same gusty night,
> The same autumn season—
> I brew my life into sweet wine
> and offer, repeatedly, to your sweet lips,
> A toast,
> A second and a third,
>
> I've sighed each night since then
>
> with the dripping rains . . .
> I've cried each day since then,
> and watched the falling leaves;
> Since then I write my poems
> Drearily, drearily . . .[7]

In the light of these somewhat maudlin expressions, it is hardly surprising that Feng came to denounce the sentimentality of his early poetic efforts in his later years. In the preface to *Feng Chih shih-wen hsüan-chih* (*Selected Poems and Prose of Feng Chih*), he confesses that the works written prior to 1930 express "narrow sentiments" and are the "personal lamentations of a bored youth."[8]

In spite of the severe assessment which Feng has leveled on his early attempts, many of those works, like those of Pien Chih-lin, contain striking metaphors and images which provided the impetus for a movement away from the poetics characteristically associated with European romanticism. Pien Chih-lin, who is a far more capable modernist than Li Chin-fa, for instance, presents pictorial perspectives by juxtaposing images in lines, such as:

> You stand on the bridge watching
>   the scenery,
> Someone watching the scenery in the
>   pavilion watches you.
> The bright moon decorates your window,
> You decorate another's dream.[9]

Works such as Feng Chih's "Southern Night" marked a milestone in Chinese lyricism inasmuch as their restrained diction and contemplative tone became distinctive characteristics of this new school of poetry. The tension which binds "Southern Night," according to Ho Ch'i-fang, surpasses that of love,[10] while another critic hails this poem as the most "modern poem" to be written along traditional lines.[11] Along with Pien Chih-lin's "White Conch," Feng's poems, particularly "Southern Night," have come to be regarded as the origins of the metaphysical trend in modern Chinese poetry. Although a new approach to poetics was introduced in these metaphysical poems, their mysticism was very much in keeping with the age-old mysticism of Buddhism and Taoism. In summarizing the elements of this new mysticism, Hsü Kai-yu notes that the new metaphysics " . . . analyzed and metaphorized with an equal degree of detachment."[12] The extent to which humanity, the universe and love are scrutinized in the poems of Feng and Pien is seen in the fact that their works often lay bare" . . . the ingredients of their ideas . . . , the basic components of their conceptual world," and therewith,their assumptions regarding " . . . the existence of the soul, the dichotomy of form and matter, ultimate reality and primary cause."[13]

Southern Night

> We sit quietly beside the lake
> And listen to swallows telling
>   the quiet night of the South.
> The Southern quiet night is brought in
>   by them—
> Evening reeds evaporating poignant passions;
>   I am intoxicated in the Southern night's air,
>   Wishing you could smell the reed's fragrance.
>
> You say the Great Bear is often like the polar bear,

Your whole body shivers as you watch.
At this moment, swallows slanting slightly o'er
    the water,
All stars in the lake are stirred—
    Please look at the lake's stars,
    The same phenomenon is the starry night of
      the South.

You say you are suspicious about the white pine,
As if the snow on its trunk has not melted.
At this moment, a swallow soars to a palm,
Singing in a flaming tone:
    Please listen to the swallows' songs,
    The same phenomenon is the forest of
      the South.

We still feel we are not the people of the South,
Our hearts are often filled with
    wintry indifference.
The swallow says, there is a rare flower
    in the South,
Blooming after twenty years of solitude—
Suddenly I feel a flower hidden in my heart
Bursting like fires in the quiet night![14]

In "Southern Night," through the subtle modulations created by
Feng's adroit phrasing, images telescope into each other and finally
extend to the poem's central image of the flower in the poet's heart.
A general view of the nocturnal scene is first presented, and by
gradations other scenic frames merge to create a flower of passion,
which replaces the darkness of the "quiet night" with "bursting
fires."

The language of the entire poem is characterized by a measured
sobriety, but in keeping with the symbolic expression of passion's
outburst in the image of the red flower, there is a sense of explo-
siveness in the exclamatory tone of the closing couplet. Form and
content are thus perfectly integrated in terms of "passion dissolving
into reason," for although love and passion are the poem's central
theme, there is none of the highly subjective sentimentality which
characterizes so many of the poems composed by Chinese poets of
the period. In Feng's hands, language becomes an apt vehicle of
psychic drama, lending shape, color, texture and impact to the
otherwise ephemeral movements of the mind.

Likewise, we find the skillful integration of external reality with the imagination in Pien Chih-lin's poem "White Conch":

> You, white conch, empty and spiritual,
> Spotless are the holes.
> Once I hold it in my hands,
> It creates in me a thousand feelings:
> In my palm,
> Waves dashing and roaring;
> Oh, great sea,
> I admire your crafty design—
> Your waves are as delicate as
>   a string of pearls!
> And yet I cannot but wonder:
> Such cleanliness!
>
> Look how I soak myself
> Like a wet bird's feather
> In a lake of misty rains.
> I feel like an attic
> With winds, willow catkins
>   passing through,
> And swallows shuttle.
> Some rare books, perhaps,
> In the attic
> With silverfish swimming among pages—
> Diving from the word "love"
> Into "grief."
> Wouldn't it be better
> to emerge from this worldly emptiness!
>
> Little white conch, how lovely!
> Me?
> The sea sends me to the beach,
> In case I fall into human hands,
> I hope that I may be favored
> by primitive men:
> To exchange me for a goat
> as one-fifteenth of the deal;
> Or I may be worth just a peach.
> And yet I worry:
> Should I be picked up
> By an imaginative thinker—
> You, white conch, empty and spiritual,
> Arouse my tides of grief:

I dream of your past,
Stony stairs, worn down by
drops from the eaves;
Well curbs, sawed off by
tugs of the rope;
Time wears through in patience!
Yellow are the fledgelings,
Green, the tiny parasol trees,
And rosy, the roses.
But when you look back to the roadside,
Your night tears are still hanging
On the tender thorns of the eglantine.[15]

In this work, a shift in narrative perspectives between the poet's voice and the poet speaking as the white conch is used to project the concept of reality and the mind's role in shaping reality. In the first stanza, the poet's voice is heard as it muses over the "empty, spiritual" white conch. As he sees the myriad of tiny openings in the shell, his mind is, figuratively, drawn into the shell itself, and he begins to experience "a thousand feelings." From his initially detached perspective, the poet is able to view the physical characteristics of the conch. By permitting his imagination to take over his human identity via his "entry" into the shell, a separate and distinctly different view, namely that of the shell, is presented to the poet.

From the poet's perspective, the white conch becomes a symbol of the ultimate spiritual purity which is arrived at only through the cleansing and eroding processes imposed by the external world. From the perspective presented by the white conch, however, we learn of the actual pain associated with this process. The shell compares itself, for instance, to an attic (a place traditionally associated, incidentally, with the past, the obsolete and removal from human society), where wind passes through and swallows shuttle back and forth. The shell's desire is that it might fall into the hands of some primitive tribe and be used as a medium of commercial exchange, to be worth "one-fifteenth of the total deal," or "just a peach."

What emerges from these dual perspectives is an understanding that although spiritual purity, and consequently, detachment from the world, is highly desirable, some aspect of the human mind still desires contact with the activities of the world. It is this aspect of humanity that desires to be of some worth, no matter how small, in completely human, and thus, physical terms. In the closing stanza, the poet's voice speaks again, describing metaphorically the effects of past tasks associated with the quest for spiritual purity, "stony stairs worn down by/drops from the eaves," "well curbs sawed off by/tugs of the rope." The implied resolution in the closing lines suggests that although human desires run counter to ascetic demands, an individual should respond to human inclinations. To do so would be as natural as the return of yellow to the fledgelings, green to the parasol trees and "rosiness" to the roses. The isolation and absence of human contact suggested by the image of the attic, Pien seems to say, must give way to the natural desire for social interaction. In the context of time's progression, the hardships of the ascetic life seem as futile and precarious as "night tears" hanging "on the tender thorns of the eglantine."

Although two perspectives are presented in terms of the "you" of the conch and the "I" of the poet, these pronouns are used less as an indication of two separate personalities than as dual views of the same issue. Diagrammatically, the contrast between Feng Chih's narrative structure in "Southern Night" and the "personae" of Pien's "White Conch" can be illustrated, as follows:

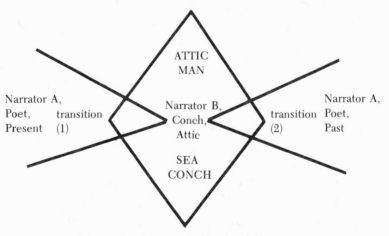

Transition (1): "Little white conch, how lovely!"
Transition (2): "I dream of your past,/Stony stairs . . ."

While Pien Chih-lin's works are often characterized by compressed images with ambiguous implications, Feng Chih's lyric
strength lies in the clarity of his expressions and the subtlety with
which these expressions are voiced. This precision of Feng's
metaphors in clarifying his central themes is perhaps best dem-
onstrated in his poem "Snake."

> My loneliness, a long snake,
> Mute, silent.
> If you, by chance, should dream of it,
> Don't ever be afraid.
>
> It is my faithful companion,
> Whose heart is sick
> with feverish nostalgia;
> It dreams of the luxuriant prairie—
> Your head's dark, thick hair.
>
> Soft as the moonlight, it swiftly
> Glides to you,
> Bringing you a dream
> Like a pink flower held in its mouth.[16]

The image of the snake with its traditional associations with evil
seems an unlikely one for a poem of longing. However, it soon
becomes evident that the poet's loneliness and yearning, extending
themselves with wave-like movements into the space which sepa-
rates him from his beloved, is best expressed verbally by the movements of a snake, since loneliness is essentially an abstraction. The
psychological tenor of this poem is heightened by the dream-like
image of loneliness: a snake bearing the pink flower of love in its
mouth and gliding silently across time and space into the dream
consciousness of the poet's beloved. In spite of the obvious intensity
of the poet's longing, there is, by the same token, a sense of restraint
which is conveyed both by the image of progression and retraction
in the snake's movements and in the verb "hsien" which is used in
conjunction with the pink flower of love in the closing stanza. The
word "hsien" can mean to hold in the mouth, but it can also mean to
control, or the bit used in horsemanship. Hence, although the
poet's passion is stirred in his loneliness by "feverish nostalgia," it is
carefully bridled by love, not a love symbolized by the "flower of the

south/ . . .that wants to bloom like fires in this quiet night," but by
the somewhat more pristine pink flower.

In "Fig," which has come to represent Feng's statement of his
own early works, the notion of a vivified or "fruitful poem" as not
having need of elaborate embellishments is seen in the metaphor of
the fig which bears fruit without having flowers.

> Look at this brown, shadowy, unripe fruit:
> It never blossoms with pink flowers
> like my longing for you; many poems
> have been written,
> but we each have not loved like a flower.

> If you would like to taste it, please do so!
> There is no comparing it with your
> beloved peach, pear or apple:
> My poem is not euphonic,
> When you read it,
> your tongue will feel it bite.[17]

In presenting the differences which lie between his own compositions and those of other poets, Feng appeals to the senses to evoke
these distinctions. Unlike the "pink flowers of love" felt between the
poet and his beloved, the poetics he bears are neither pleasing to
the ear nor the palate. There is an awareness on the poet's part of his
own distinctiveness, for in addressing the poem to his beloved,
Feng says that they have yet to love "another such flower," or, in
other words, to enjoy poetry akin to Feng's compositions. Human
love in terms of pink flowers, Feng seems to add, is pleasant
enough, but poems such as those Feng creates, with their unembel-
lished harshness and dark, sinister undertones, have yet to be
widely accepted on their own terms.

In comparison to poets who wrote in the era of the Sino-Japanese
war, Feng's spirit of nationalism seems to have remained at a fairly
even keel. While patriotism rose to vehement heights in the poetry
of several of his compatriots, Feng's own works hardly reflect the
chaos of his milieu. During the Sino-Japanese war of 1937–45, most
poets retreated with the Nationalist government to Kunming,
where many taught at the National Southwest Associated University. They found it necessary to create new poetic devices and styles
to accomodate the prevalent nationalistic spirit. Even poets like

Pien Chih-lin abandoned the obscurity of their highly symbolic images in favor of direct and concise expression. Pien's epistolary poems, for example, which he dedicated to compatriots fighting the war, are characterized by a crispness quite uncharacteristic of his earlier works.

Feng Chih's sense of nationalism (at least in its poetic expression) remained unstirred during the Sino-Japanese war, but there is evidence that he was not totally unaware of social issues. As early as 1926, for instance, his poem "Evening Paper," with its dedication to "a boy selling newspapers," reveals a painful awareness of social injustice and human degradation. The poem itself is reminiscent of Blake's social comment in the two poems on "The Chimney Sweeper," and Feng's work has definite romantic overtones, particularly in the poet's subjective view of the newspaper boy. He identifies himself with the paper boy's plight of having to sell papers on the streets of Peking at midnight.

> On the long streets of Peking at midnight,
> Gusty winds accompany your exhausted cries,
> "Evening paper! Evening paper! Evening paper!"
> No one opens his door—
> My heart cries out at the same time
> "Love! Love! Love!"
>
> We are both melancholy in the same way,
> Both on the same bleak rail.
> "Evening paper! Evening paper! Evening paper!"
> No one opens his door—
> Shimmering shadows fall on the dust,
> "Love! Love! Love!"
>
> Rolls and rolls in your arms—
> When the wind grows chilly,
> you hold them close to you.
> "Evening paper! Evening paper! Evening paper!"
> No one opens his door—
> Rolls of papers in my arms,
> "Love! Love! Love!"[18]

In Feng's vision, both poet and paper boy are the means by which the lives and experiences of other human beings are communicated. But human hearts " . . . are often filled with wintry indifference" to the plight of others. This painful awareness is conveyed by the image of the closed door and the cry "Evening paper! Evening paper!" which the poet sees as a cry for love and compassion. The papers clutched by the boy are only important if the accounts of human misery are communicated to others, Feng seems to say. Likewise, with its insights into the inner experience, poetry is valid only as it reaches the consciousness of others. In both instances, human indifference reduces news and poetry to mere printed paper to be clutched in moments of discomfort and anguish.

Although Feng does incorporate his geographical and social milieu in his poems, they are never dealt with strictly in their own terms. Feng spent the greater part of his life in Peking, but the physical realities of the city are only incidental to the meanings or implications with which the poet invests them. By contrast, we see the preoccupation with the details of the city proper in Lin Keng's "Era," where there are:

> Grey tents in the city;
> With the trampling of
> the Eight Nations' Army Coalition,
> the silver ingots which were buried
> have disappeared;
> The clatter of horses' hoofs on the pitch road . . .
> No longer Chinese.[19]

Feng's distance in his poetry from the realities of his immediate surroundings is matched by his independence in the face of shifting popular sentiment during the war years. Thus, although "Evening Paper" essentially involves a social issue, it lacks the intense concern with true-to-life issues as such which characterized the works of the time. Ho Ch'i-fang's "The Remnants of 'Northern China Are Burning'" is fixed in the realities of the Japanese imperialist invasion, and the precision with which Ho presents his account of a city under siege has all the journalistic explicitness of camera verité.[20]

It is Feng Chih's detachment from the details of his surroundings that perhaps distinguishes him as a romantic in the purest European sense. Northrop Frye has pointed out that "the romancer does not attempt to create 'real people' so much as stylized figures which expand into psychological archetypes."[21] For Feng, as we have already seen, the external truths, and his poetic presentation of these truths, are only important as means of conveying the movements of the inner world. In the same romantic vein, Feng, like his European counterparts, is " . . .less interested in exposing reality than in embellishing it"[22] with his own perspective of the world. Although Frye and Henry Levin refer specifically to the psychology of the romantic novelist, it is the same creative frame of mind which impels the romantic poet like Feng. Thus, when "the click of the mind's shutter" attempts to capture images of the external world, it inevitably ends up as an impressionistic and highly subjective painting.[23]

For Feng Chih, the realization of "another world" eventually came with the establishment of the People's Republic of China in 1949, but with the new regime came a new dilemma to confront Feng and his fellow poets. In keeping with Communist ideology, art could no longer exist on its own terms but had to serve as a means of educating the masses. Writers like Ai Ch'ing, Ting Ling, Hu Feng, and Feng Hsueh-feng found the notion repelling, but their rebellion was to result only in their being declared *persona non grata* by hard-line party critics.

In recent years, those poems by Feng Chih which have been allowed to circulate outside of the People's Republic of China have tended to mystify critics as to his real poetic intentions. In a confession written sometime between 1950 and 1958 during a so-called period of personal adjustment, Feng not only vigorously denounced his past works, but also critically condemned his own lack of vision. He deemed the poems of his younger days "pallid and weak, dim and stale,"[24] entirely lacking in the necessary revolutionary zeal for change. The Great Leap Forward, Feng added, with its stress on the power of the masses, would have been quite incomprehensible to him in the past.

This condemnation of his past works, coupled with his humble confession of personal failings can, and perhaps must, be approached with caution in the light of the pressures which were exerted on artists with "bourgeois inclinations" by the Communist regime. In Feng's case, his confessions could well be taken as a sincere disavowal of past views and failings, but they could also have been a means of protecting himself from the party-line purges which descended on so many of his fellow poets. As Ch'en Shih-hsiang observes in "Metaphor and the Conscious in Chinese Poetry," the apologetic tenor of Feng's recent writings reveals a "strained consciousness and over-attentiveness as when one keeps vigil at night."[25]

From the literary standpoint, Feng's recent works indicate his inability to establish a system of poetics which could incorporate ideology and artistic sense. Under the pressures of having to compose works which meet the specifications of Communist dictums, Feng's works have tended to take on both a self-accusing air, bordering on the masochistic, and a tone of strident assertiveness which so often characterizes propaganda pieces.

In a work which could well have been written to protect himself against an accusation of self-centeredness, Feng writes:

> There was a naive poet
> Who wanted to see heaven in a wild flower;
> A wild flower is indeed pretty,
> But his heaven seems too vague.[26]

To a large extent, this poem represents a complete departure from Feng's early efforts, where lyricism and the poet's own sensitivities shaped and directed his creations. Artistically, Feng's departure from his lyricism has resulted in works which, sadly, border on cant. In an enthusiastic renunciation of his own heritage, and an equally enthusiastic embracing of Maoist thought he writes:

> Since I was born of my parents
> My heart was covered with dust.
> In all these years,
> I buried myself deeper,
> As on a tedious, wintry night,
> Perceiving neither morning nor spring.
>
> Day and night you shine on me,
> Shining on everyone in the motherland.
> You are the party, you are Chairman Mao,
> You are my parents reborn,
> You are my everlasting benefactor.[27]

The acceptance of party-line doctrines did not, in Feng's case, only lead to self-denunciation. In the year when Ai Ch'ing and Ting Ling were purged, Feng lashed out against the "egotistic view of life" which he deemed a product of capitalism. In a scathing criticism of Ai Ch'ing, who, when questioned, replied, "A writer only sees things according to his *Weltanschaung*,"[28] Feng asks: What kind of *Weltanschaung* is Ai Ch'ing's *Weltanschaung*? What kind of emotions are Ai Ch'ing's emotions? From his essay we know that it is a capitalistic, egotistic *Weltanschaung* and emotion.[29]

The divergence of poetic styles between the early and later stages of Feng Chih's poetic career, makes it hard for us to switch all our attention to his later productions, despite Feng's strong insistence. We could assert that the emergence of the "new ballads" and the ideological unification of Revolutionary Romanticism and Revolutionary Realism have turned Feng's attention to the socialist endeavor. Nevertheless, his poetic achievements should be viewed differently at various stages and in the context of political ideologies.

CHAPTER 3

The Sonneteer

I The Sonnet Form

THE sonnet form in Chinese poetry has been directly borrowed from an essentially European literary form by modern Chinese poets. One Chinese word for sonnet, *shih-ssu-hang*, literally means a fourteen-line poem, while its other name, *shang-lai*, is simply a phonetic transcription of the English word "sonnet." The fourteen-line verse form with its variously divided rhyme patterns was, therefore, not a Chinese form until its adoption by Chinese poets who had, in one way or another, been exposed to European literature.

Beyond using the basic fourteen-line structure, Chinese poets, for the most part, have seldom attempted to follow the accepted rhyme patterns of either the Petrarchan or Shakespearean sonnet forms. For them, any modern poem in fourteen lines could be called a "'sonnet."

In Feng Chih's case, there is even a denial altogether of a conscious borrowing from the West: it was merely the convenience of a fourteen-line structure that led Feng to use it as a vehicle for his poetic expressions. The form itself, while providing the poet with a circumscribed arena in which to work, is sufficiently flexible to allow for a fairly wide sweep of the imagination. In Li Kuang-t'ien's words, the form has allowed for a sense of rising and falling in consecutive layers, a concentration and dispersal of themes and images and an interweaving of rhymes throughout the fabric of Feng's poems. Other than the fact that his poems all consist of fourteen lines, the only resemblance Feng's work bears to the Petrarchan sonnet is in the division of his verse into octaves and sestets. None of Feng's poems conform to the rhyming patterns of the Shakespearean sonnet.

41

Feng has managed to overcome the difficulties unique to the Chinese language regarding the placement of stressed and unstressed syllables by having all of his lines conform to the same number of syllables. By doing so, he stabilizes his metrical patterns. A large proportion of his sonnets have deca-syllabic lines which conform roughly to the five pairs of bi-syllabic words of the English pentameter. Thus, when all his lines are of the same length (in several instances, alternate lines have the same number of syllables), Feng allows for pauses which therefore occur at established intervals. The regularly spaced intervals set up a very definite pattern of phrases and pauses which correspond to the stressed and unstressed syllables of Western poetry. When variations to the number of syllables occur in each line, Feng regulates the pauses by the ordered arrangement of ten- and nine- syllable lines in pairs which may either follow each other consecutively or alternate with one another. In Sonnet One, for instance, we find the following arrangement of lines:

> 10 syllables
> 9 syllables
> 10 syllables
> 9 syllables
>
> 10 syllables
> 10 syllables
> 10 syllables
> 10 syllables
>
> 9 syllables
> 9 syllables
> 9 syllables
>
> 10 syllables
> 10 syllables
> 9 syllables

The pause at the end of those lines with nine syllables will obviously occur sooner than with the ten-syllable lines, but by alternating the two a rhythmic pattern (which is different certainly from that found in a poem consistently having ten syllables throughout) based on the pauses at the end of each line emerges.

An analysis of the rhyme patterns in his sonnets reveals variety rather than uniformity.[2] None of his sonnets conforms to either the *abba abba cde cde* of the Petrarchan scheme or to the abab cdcd ef ef gg of Shakespeare's design. In the major portion of Feng's sonnets, an *abba* scheme is employed in the opening quatrain, followed by a diverse combination of rhyme patterns.

While the presentation, exposition and resolution of the poet's vision are aligned in terms of the structural divisions in the European sonnets, Feng's thoughts by way of contrast are never bounded by the octave and sestet. In Sonnet Ten, dedicated to the educator Ts'ai Yuan-p'ei, Feng links the last lines in the octave and the first line of the following sestet, rather than allowing an artificial separation to occur.

On several occasions, these enjambments are simply the continuations of ideas which have extended beyond the limitations imposed by the structural delineations of the sonnet. In Sonnet Eleven, dedicated to Lu Hsun, Feng speaks of him as a "protector" who "throughout his life [was] rejected by this world." The line "Its protector was, throughout his life" is the last line of the octave and should, ostensibly, be a summation of the poem's central thesis. Feng is therefore caught, so to speak, at a point in the poem with an idea which is, as yet, uncompleted. His only recourse is the enjambment which runs into the sestet portion of the sonnet. Likewise, in poems where an amplification of the poem's subject through a series of itemizations occurs, Feng continues his descriptions beyond the boundaries dictated by the divisions of the Petrarchan sonnet. In Sonnet Fourteen, the passion of van Gogh (to whom it is dedicated) is manifest in a variety of objects, such as sun flowers, cypresses and "People walking/Beneath the scorching sun." By placing a premium on the urgent continuity these images evoke, Feng must allow for the enjambment between the line "People walking" and the first line of the second quatrain which contains the words "Beneath the scorching sun." Later in the same sonnet, a second enjambment between the last line of the octave and the following line again occurs as a result of the continuation of a single thought pattern.

It is this vision of thought as an organic movement which "runs towards the infinite," that finally sets Feng's sonnets apart from the traditional Western sonnet, where thought is carefully pared down to fit the limitations of form. For Feng Chih, form becomes simply a bottle which temporarily captures the "flow of the shapeless water" (Sonnet Twenty-seven) while lending it its own shape. Presumably, even while held in an enclosed structure (to continue the analogy of the water bottle), a poem's inner movements cannot be hampered or permitted to solidify into a rigid mass. In his last sonnet, Feng uses the image of the weather vane as a metaphor for the poetic form he has adopted. The movements of the mind, Feng implies, are as invisible as the wind. The vane, fluttering in the autumn wind, exists not to bring attention to itself but as a means of indicating the directions taken by the wind. By analogy, the sonnet form, in Feng's hands, becomes simply an indicator of the imagination's movements, a means whereby the poet's inner thoughts are formalized and made manifest.

II *The Orphic Imagery*

The poet's use of the material world to symbolize the abstract is, in European literature, rooted in classical mythology. As Walter Strauss indicates in his study of the Orphic myth in modern literature, romanticism, and in particular German romanticism, as a mode of thought, attempted to reconcile the mechanized view of the Age of Reason with the validity of the nonrational and intangible aspects of human experience. In redefining the poet, the Orphic myth provides a mode by which the poet, " . . . disposed by ages of cold reason" could recover "his own domain as soothsayer, harmonizer . . . and legislator."[3] Strauss adds that " . . . the decisive factor in appraising the nature of the modern poet as Orpheus is not so much in the magical mission of the poet, but in the account and interpretation of his experience as reflected in his poetry."[4]

This mythic experience of the artistic process, curiously enough, generated Feng Chih's collection of twenty-seven sonnets. Although no evidence exists to show that Feng was aware of Rainer Maria Rilke's use of the myth in his *Sonnets to Orpheus*, we know with certainty that Feng was familiar with Rilke and the German romantic tradition. Feng Chih received his doctorate in 1935 from the University of Berlin and translated Rilke's *Letters to a Young Poet*, which was published in 1948. Reading Pien Chih-lin's translation of Rilke's *The Lay of the Love and Death of Cornet Christopher Rilke* in 1942, Feng was sufficiently impressed by the poetic narrative to rearrange his own version of the classical legend of Wu Tzu-hsu along the lines of Rilke's novella.

No direct reference is ever made in Feng Chih's collection of sonnets to either Orpheus or the Orphic myth, but the distinguishing features of the Orphic myth as a metaphor of the creative process are, nevertheless, evident in this particular collection of poems. In the preface to the second edition of his sonnets, Feng hinted that in the year 1939 or 1940 he had gone through a particular kind of mystical experience, the result of which was the creation of the sonnets.[5] This reminds us of Rilke's letter describing the completion of his sonnets "as the most mysterious . . .enigmatic dictations."[6] It is therefore quite natural to discover, from time to time, parallels to Rilke's work emerging in various sonnets, disguised by an undeniably Chinese sensitivity and a tinge of contemporary patriotism, but still retaining the strong imprint of German romanticism.

During a sojourn to Heidelberg in 1935, Feng Chih, walking in the hills with a book, experienced a sense of enlightenment as he read the famous couplet by the poet Chia Tao, "Walking alone, shadow under the pond/Resting for a few moments, body against the tree." Feng then felt as if every word " . . . contained in the couplet had been transformed into each blade of grass and every tree."[7]

This experience undoubtedly brings to mind that of Rilke in the garden of Schloss Duino where the German poet encountered "the other side of nature." In 1912, Rilke "happened to recline into the more or less shoulder high fork of a shrub-like tree." While in this position, he slipped into a somnambulistic state and began perceiving vibrations passing from the tree to himself. On being questioned as to the significance of this experience, Rilke replied to himself that he must have "arrived on the other side of nature."[8]

Both instances (the Rilke phrase "reclined against a tree" and Feng Chih's quote of Chia Tao's couplet, "body against a tree") could be viewed as an identification of the self with a natural object. This particularly illustrates the concept of an Orphic tree, the body of the self projecting and integrating with the body of the tree, and establishing a cohesive existence with it. The Orphic poet aims at an integration of the self with the world around him, and at the same time, aims at a reconciliation of all opposites. Drawing a parallel between these traditions, Feng Chih makes the body resting against the tree analogous to "a butterfly resting on a flower, on which the life of the butterfly mingles with the color and fragrance of the flower, as does the human body and the trunk of a tree."[9] The mingling of the "life" of a subject with the "color and fragrance" of an intended object, the juxtaposition of the butterfly and the flower, strongly suggests the aesthetic experience of the *haiku* poet

Moritake, who once described this ambiguity in his poem: "A falling flower, thought I,/ Fluttering back to the branch—/ Was a butterfly."[10] Thus, we see that the butterfly here possesses a dual existence as a flower (in the mind of the poet) and a butterfly (in reality). The body leaning against a tree, in Feng Chih's terms, metaphorically implies that:

from our blood circulations we can feel how a tree draws nourishment from the soil and transfuses it to branches and leaves. Even our blood seems to be transfused. (Rilke has an article relating his experience of how he reclined against a tree and the tree spirit diffused into his body.) This is not a union with nature, but rather arranging oneself in a situation so that one can communicate with nature.[11]

How does such arrangement or mingling take place? In both experiences (Feng Chih's enlightenment with his poetic environment and Rilke's empathy with a tree), the poets were alone and immersed in a semi-waking state. A sense of the merging of all things was felt and identities converged. Inner and outer world flowed one into the other, undefined, seemingly, by divisions created by the conscious application of words and structures. Feng Chih opens his sonnets with this state of preparedness:

> We are ready to receive profoundly,
> Unexpected mysteries,
> In these prolix times; the sudden appearance
> of a comet, the whirling, gusty wind:
>
> At this very moment, our lives
> Are in the first embrace,
> Joys and sorrows come quickly to our eyes
> Solidifying into towering forms.[12]

(Feng , Sonnet One)

The meanings of things and the deeper significance of occurences in life do not, however, merge at the moment the poet encounters the thing or specific event, but rather, during moments of solitude, when a fusion of the spirit with the environment occurs and the poet conceives the whirling wind and the coming comet. The poet uses the symbol of the "sky-piercing tower"—the tree, in Sonnet Two, to depict the extent to which "the things close to us" must be stripped off themselves to reveal layer upon layer of meaning. The constant search and the process of comprehending these layers of meaning inevitably involves the shifting of identities. Rilke emphasized this in a sonnet, pleading with his audience to:

> Erect no monument. But let the roses
> blossom every year for his memory's sake.
> For it is Orpheus. His metamorphosis
> into this one and that. We need not take
>
> trouble for other names. Once and for all,
> it's Orpheus when there's song. He comes and goes.
> Is it not much if sometimes a few days
> he outlives the roses in the bowl?[13]
>
> (Rilke, Sonnet Five)

The "towering forms" or the songs of Orpheus can thus be viewed as a convergence of objects and memories of past experiences able to transcend destructive time. The moment of realization, however, eludes the poet's grasp, and with Feng Chih, the brief encounter can only be described in terms of "tiny insects/ Braving the conjugation./ Resisting imminent danger/ Their wondrous lives brought to an end" (Feng, Sonnet One). With Rilke, in order to make the song Orphic, the poet has to wander forever in the realms of life and death. The audience could not but "fear this evanescence./ For while his word surpasses this existence,/ he's gone alone already in the distance" (Rilke, Sonnet Five).

Significantly, in Feng's sonnets the tree, with its roots reaching deep into the earth and its branches rising and dividing towards the sky, becomes the symbol of the Orphic process. As the Orphic-tree imagery implies, the growth of a tree involves the double realm Orpheus alone travels. In quest of his lost love, Eurydice, Orpheus went down to the underworld, the realm of darkness, to bring Eurydice back to the human world. The descent into death and the return to life is typical of the tree symbol found in Feng Chih and Rilke. The penetrating roots searching for a pure but dark center is the heroic quest of Orpheus descending to, and becoming reconciled with, death. What is nourished from the roots of the tree does not remain underground but is exemplified above ground. The return of Orpheus is often marked by his new song of past experiences. The "rising tree" in Rilke and the "sky-piercing tower" in Feng can be looked upon as the ascent consequential to the roots' descent.

The double realm, therefore, signifies the principle of double-death and double-life which is the gist of Feng's and Rilke's belief in the metamorphosis. According to Rilke, the versatile poet is the only one who travels back and forth through the realms of life and death and whose artistry lies in the following question and answer—"Does he belong here? No, from both/ realms his ample nature has grown./ One to whom the roots were known/ could bend more deftly the willow's growth" (Rilke, Sonnet Six). The willow refers to the willow bough Orpheus carried as a talisman to the underworld. It also symbolizes Orpheus's deterministic attitude (the soft, yielding nature of the willow bough) towards the second loss of his wife. Walter Strauss has commented on this attitude in contrast with the Promethean hero: "Prometheanism aims for an outer transformation of society; it proposes to ameliorate man's lot by external action. Orphism proposes to transmute the inner man by a confrontation with himself and to alter society only indirectly, through the changes that man can effect within himself. All of modern literature tends to fall within the area delimited by these two points of reference, rebellion and refusal."[14] Only if we understand the dual existence of life and death, descent and return, can we comprehend the nonrebellious Orphic refusal. Earlier in the Duino elegies, Rilke had insisted on such reciprocity in asking "O Tree of life, when will your winter come?/ We're never single-minded, unperplexed,/ like migratory birds, outstrip and late,/ We suddenly thrust into the wind, and fall/ into unfeeling ponds. We comprehend/ flowering and fading simultaneously."[15] This Orphic attitude is shared by Feng Chih in his metamorphic treatment of the eucalyptus tree. The poet praises the soughing jade tree rising like "the body of a saint before me,/ Sanctify a clamorous city" together with its "constantly shedding" of the bark amidst the withering season. The rising movement is further complemented by the poet's wish to die "by inches/ . . . covered by your roots" (Feng, Sonnet Three). Thus, we see death appearing to both Feng and Rilke not as terminal, but as a stage of departure to a more profound internal world. In a sonnet addressed to Goethe, Feng Chih relates the moth plunging into fire and snakes shedding their skins to the German poet's creed of "Death and metamorphosis" (Feng, Sonnet Thirteen). Like the Orphic tree in Rilke's poem which flowers and fades simultaneously, the withering tree in Feng's sonnets demonstrates a unique Orphic sense of yielding harmony. The poet arranges himself in time like "Autumn trees, each/ Offering leaves and belated blossoms/ to the autumn wind, that our/ trunks may stretch into frigid winters" (Feng, Sonnet Two).

When Orpheus sings, the animals come to listen, "And all was still." These animals came "from the silence, from the clear/now opened wood came forth from nest and den;" (Rilke, Sonnet One). Silence is indispensable before the listening because it enhances the sensibility of each personal reception, and is thus directly responsible for every self-transformation. The diverging concept of silence and solitude between Rilke and Feng Chih is worth noting. Rilke assumes an almost ascetic attitude in attaining his internal silence. He tells his friends in one of his letters that "there is but one solitude, and that is great, and not easy to bear, and to almost everybody come hours when they would gladly exchange it for any sort of intercourse, however banal and cheap . . ."[16] In the preface to his translation of the *Letters to a Young Poet*, Feng Chih describes silence and loneliness in terms of garden trees: "their branches and leaves may echo each other, but roots that penetrate deeply into the earth for nourishment are quite irrelevant to each other. Each of them is silent and alone."[17] Again, this positive disintegration is further substantiated in his sonnet in praise of Venice:

> I shall never forget
> That water city of the West,
> Symbol of the human world,
> Conglomerate of a thousand loneliness.
>
> Each an island
> Each seeking a friend in another.
> Your hand touches mine,
> A bridge across the water.

> (Feng, Sonnet Five)

With Rilke, the reconciliation is found in the hearing. Once the song is made, and listened to, there is change and transformation. According to Ovid, as Orpheus made his song, beasts came out from their caves and trees appeared to form a forest. Yet with Rilke, the real meaning lies in the "pure transcension" of the music. It is the "tall tree in the ear" that "made for the beasts temples in the hearing" (Rilke, Sonnet One). It is the music that makes a forest, not trees.

In Feng Chih's third sonnet, the internal "listening" whose " . . . countermotif is Orpheus's singing,"[18] finds expression in the distinctly Chinese image of the jade tree. While listening to the wind in its branches, the poet finds that the sounds soon cease to exist as physically audible sounds but are transformed into a "solemn temple of music." That which is essentially perceived by the senses has become a transcendent "temple" in the poet's imagination. Having undergone this transformation, the music once more solidifies into a visible "sky-piercing tower." Once this process has taken place, the tree is no longer simply an object in nature. For Feng Chih, it becomes "a saint," its existence a symbol of both the transformation in the poetic process, as well as the regeneration of death to which the creative mind must constantly be subjected.

Thus, the use of the tree as a pictorial representation of the Orphic process is implicit in several of Feng Chih's sonnets, although Orpheus is never mentioned and no direct references are made to the myth. The focus of Feng's poems, therefore, is not the myth itself, but rather the meanings suggested by the myth. Elizabeth Sewell's observation that the Orphic poet is "not a gusher of imagery and sentiments . . .his thinking is strictly in lyric, in concentratedly poetic, mythological terms,"[19] applies to Feng Chih's use of the Orphic myth.

III   The Contemplative Process

"Walking alone, shadow under the pond,
Resting for a few moments, body against the tree."
                                        Chia Tao (777–841)

Feng Chih believed that all the experiences he encountered in his life, regardless of their significance, not only had meaning in and of themselves, but also suggested a philosophy relating to life as a whole. Such a belief is founded on an ability to view the objects and experiences encountered not only in terms of themselves, but also in terms of their representing the ideas of themselves. William

Carlos Williams insists that ideas do not exist save in things, and it is this search for underlying meanings and the direction of these underlying meanings towards an ardent patriotism that characterizes the sonnets of Feng Chih.

The combined acts of looking and thinking are, for Feng Chih, crucial to the discovery of new meanings. On his solitary walks he says that "a person alone on mountain paths cannot help but look and think."[20] The act of looking and thinking involves the integration of the external environment with past experiences and perceptions. "Which wind or cloud does not call to the other?"[21] Feng asks, and a pine tree on a distant slope catalyzes thoughts and provokes questions. In expressing both the external and the internal, the poet must resort not only to conscious thought but also to the regions of imagination the poet Chia Tao referred to as the "shadow under the pond." Traditionally, Chinese poets recognize a certain quiescence of the spirit, or an equilibrium between conscious thought and the workings of the unconscious mind, as a prerequisite for the emergence of the shadow under the transparent pond.

In Sonnet Sixteen, the shadow-pond takes shape via a series of transformations in the landscape the poet sees before him. Standing on a high peak, Feng discovers that the initially "unyielding vista" gradually yields to the synthesizing process of the poet's imagination, becoming first a "vast plain," then a plain carved with "crisscrossing paths." What is initially unyielding or too solidly material gives way to the imagination's ability to manipulate, to coax and transform all things into "bod[ies] of the light."[22] According to Williams, things in themselves are "nothing but the blank faces and cylindrical trees," their existence "forked by perception an accident,"[23] but for Feng there had to be a movement away from this narrow perception before human life in terms of society, nation and the universe could be fully understood. "Cities, mountains, and rivers we have passed/become our lives" Feng believes, suggesting that every experience illuminates past experiences and cannot be permitted to be bypassed only as "things" in life.

In an essay on Kunming entitled "The Extinct Mountain Village," Feng describes the aftermath of a deserted village:

Now, no foundation of a house could be found. Only trees, plains, and rivers are left. Except for the house in which we live, there are no other houses within a radius of four or five miles. However, each mountain, each secluded place is still left with a name. These names exist only in the mouths of woodcutters and herdsmen of the neighboring villages.[24]

To the poet, then, the city of Kunming ceases to be merely a geographical entity, a city in Yunnan province. His encounter with death, desolation and suffering as described in his essay forces him into the realization that the city's destruction and the terror it has experienced are linked to the cities which have been destroyed in the past and the suffering which will inevitably come with the holocausts of the future. Like mountains whose names are insignificant, Feng says, cities are important only if they " . . . remind us of their past relationship with men, and are hidden with a short history of their rise and fall."[25]

This capacity to look beyond present issues is linked inextricably with the choices human beings must make. For Feng, the myopia which confines perceptions to the immediate and the material must lead only to choices which will prove destructive to human beings in the larger context of history. In his search for meanings in and beyond things, Feng Chih inevitably resorts to symbolic representations of his personal vision. His symbol for the human mind is always the river, meandering obliviously toward the great sea, only to recede again on a backward course once it has reached the ocean.

In his seventh sonnet, a temporary unification of wills and goals amongst the Chinese people is seen to take place. In the face of air raids over Kunming, there is a mass exodus to a rural part of the city. For a brief span of time at least, there is a revelation amongst those huddled together in this hurried flight of the meaning of war and its peculiar place in the context of China's history, for there is:

> The same awakening
> in our hearts.
> A similar fate
> Upon our shoulders.
>
> (Sonnet Seven)

When all danger is passed, the "great sea," brought together by the threat of peril to a realization as to the meaning of this experience, again disperses, never to be united again. Anxious perhaps to return to the city to check his personal losses, the individual, as Feng Chih views the situation, again "meanders" to the spiritual myopia which clouds his daily existence:

> Diverging streets
> Again absorb us:
> Sea scattering into rivers.
>
> (Sonnet Seven)

In contrast to his use of the meandering rivers as symbols of man's divergent self-interests, Feng employs the goal-directed pathway as a representation of unified striving. In Sonnet Twenty-six, the misdirection of goals is presented metaphorically as a walk through the woods. Journeying on a path which is ordinarily familiar to him, the poet suddenly finds himself taking a strange route. The apprehension which arises soon clears as home, emerging "like a new island on the horizon," is sighted through the trees. The destination is familiar enough; it is the poet's home. Yet, as the final lines imply, "Don't feel that everything is familiar;/ Till death comes, you touch yourself/ Wondering: whose body is this?" even in something as familiar as one's own body, there lies an unknown aspect which can serve to either elevate or delude human intentions. It is here that Feng exhibits a caution generally uncharacteristic of visionaries. For having " . . . receive[d] profoundly/unexpected mysteries," Feng's vision of a unified China does not direct him along untraversed avenues but rather along paths trod by generations of Chinese before him: "Lonely children, white haired couples/ Youth./ And friends now dead./ All have walked out their paths;/ Retread these steps/ that the paths will not be left to the wilderness" (Sonnet Seventeen).

There is none of Robert Frost's desire to take the road "less travelled by," not even a parallel to the dilemma of being " . . . sorry I could not travel both/ and be one traveller."[26] Instead, there is a vision of human existence aligned against time, a vision of life as " . . . a passage of the song/ Falling from the corpus of music" (Sonnet Two), which directs Feng to its ultimate goal. In the progression of time, there can be no quest for the individual's own identity. "The benevolent heart" merges with the tears "flowing since ancient times" (Sonnet Six), and the poet himself is no different finally from the nameless country lads, the weeping village women or the nameless plants he has encountered. Only China remains, Feng's sonnets seem to say, China in an essentially hopeless universe, where a poet's vision can, perhaps, provide a moment's hope.

CHAPTER 4

The Early Growth Towards
the Narrative

THE periodic differentiation of poetic practices, and the emerging of various poetic genres, do not necessarily imply the rise and fall of a poet's creative achievements. The purpose of this chapter is to review Feng Chih's early poetic endeavors and to emphasize the parallels to his later efforts to be found there. Feng's narrative poems, particularly, reflect in his poetic career a strong potential which reinforces his abandonment of the sonnets and eventual search for the people's new ballads.

There are indications that Feng Chih started to write poetry as early as 1920, at the age of fifteen. Chang Ting-huang informs us that Feng Chih had by then written more than a thousand poems, all unpublished and limited to private circulation among close friends.[1] Later, in 1929, three of these thousand unknown pieces, "Mailman," "Inquiring" and "Thus I Sing," were finally published. The last, subtitled "Proem of The Dream Realm," is the expression of the young poet in search of his lyric kingdom:

> Leaving my mother's bosom,
> I run, towards the bosom of the universe!
> Being on such a journey,
> Thus I sing!
>
> Just leaving my mother's bosom,
> This universe seems too spacious,
> Being on such a journey,
> Thus I sing!
>
> Seeking in vain for the bosom of the universe,
> Anxiously, I am worried and confused,

> Being on such a journey,
> Thus I sing!
>
> God reveals to me my lover's bosom,
> Saying that it can lead my way.
> Being on such a journey,
> Thus I sing!
>
> For the bosom of my lover,
> Pensively I wander, everywhere,
> Being on such a journey,
> Thus I sing![2]

Although this poem represents one of Feng Chih's earliest poetic attempts, the structure and tension reflect craftsmanship that is representative of classical Chinese lyrics. The poem is divided into five stanzas of four lines each. The last couplet of each stanza is a refrain, maintaining a unity of sound and sense throughout the entire poem. The train of thought is well arranged and smoothly developed in the progression of stanzas. In the beginning, Feng plunges from maternal lineage to the spacious universe—a bold attempt to depart from his familiar environment in search of the wonders of the unknown. Realizing that his own minuteness is incompatible with the overwhelming magnificence of the universe, the poet turns to love, which mediates between human understanding and comfort. Thus, the singing is of songs of experience resulting from the failure of the search. Such a structure expresses the message of the poet and his baffling attempts to relate his experiences, and it is used in other poems under the same title; hence, "Thus I sing" presents a broad perspective of what is to come later. Since the singing, or the relating of one's experience, either happy or sad, is inseparable from the mode the singer uses, the poem demonstrates the peculiarity of such a voice. "Being on such a journey" corresponds to the impact of outer and inner experiences and leads to the creation of the rhythms required by lyric poetry. On the other hand, the combination of "Thus I sing" and "Being on such a journey," uses the convention of the narrator as a troubadour who forever plays the music of experience, both past and present.

The poem "Inquiring," written in 1921, expresses a unique contemplative quality amidst Feng Chih's love lyrics. The action takes place within the dialogue of the two lovers:

He asks his beloved:
"Do you love me?"
She replies, "I do."
Blooming are the roses near them.
He plucks one and puts it on her bosom.

Next day he asks his beloved again:
"Why do you love me?"
She replies, "I love for the love of you,
         You are my only love in this world."
Unfading are the roses near them.
He again plucks one and puts it on her bosom.

The third day he asks his beloved:
"How do you love me?"
She replies, "I love you unconditionally
         — as I love my own life."
Few remaining are the roses near them.
He plucks one and puts it on her bosom.

He finally asks his beloved:
"How are you going to love me?"
She cannot reply,
All the tears, once covered by joy, flow out!
No more are the roses, near them.[3]

As we have already seen from the previous poem, love is a revelation from God that guides the way of the baffled poet; the poet here in turn questions the validity of such a path and its permanence. When youth shines gloriously like roses blooming in their prime, the whispers of love are sweet and charming. Nevertheless, words without action, or pure indulgence in romantic fantasies, are just as feeble and ephemeral as roses, which only last a season. When roses have faded and language has lost its magical sweetness, empty promises only reveal cowardice, the failure of the will to act. When there is still youth to spend, promises are valid to the extent that they may be fulfilled in the future. When the future becomes the present, what answer, then, can she give? "She cannot reply,/ All the tears, once covered by joy, flow out!"

In "Inquiring," Feng Chih uses the glorious image of the rose to express the realization of a harsh, cold reality, but in "Mailman," he finds a correlative in the undramatic, routine comings and goings of a mailman:

> A green dressed mailman,
> walking with his head drooped;
> Looking occasionally at the sidewalks.
> His face, very common,
> His life, mostly content—
> bears no sorrow.
> Who will notice his
> walking, daily, to and fro.
> Yet his small hands are delivering
> Reality to some dreams.
> When he knocks at the door,
> Who will take note and ponder—
> "Here comes the receiver's horrendous hour."[4]

This poem, written in 1921, marked the beginning of Feng Chih's poetic career. The poet later accounted for his experience in the following recollection:

As early as 1921, when I was a youth a little short of sixteen years old, I graduated from a four-year high school, knowing not what to do in the future. The road ahead was obscure. The city of Peking was dull and grey, and everywhere were the shapes and the noises of poverty in street corners and alleys. We liked to utter a saying common to the youths at that time—"No flower, no brightness, no love." At dusk, I used to walk from one alley to the other, endlessly wandering. The black narrow door of every family in those alleys was tightly closed and the people behind those doors were unknown. I just felt that door in and door out bore the same deadly quietude.

One day, when I was wandering again, there was a mailman in green dress coming from across the alley. His face was common, serene as the silent street. His hand was holding a bundle of mail, dropping letters occasionally into the partially opened doors. Watching this, I began to think of my catastrophic country, damaged by wars and natural disasters. What kind of message could the mail have brought to these houses? What change could the mail have made for these homes? I started to trace these hollow, superficial impressions and dictated the first poem of my first poetry collection of my youthful years. My writing of poetry began like this.[5]

The unobtrusive entrance of the mailman in the poem results in a dramatic irony in that the more common and indifferent he looks, the more unexpected the bad news he carries. The juxtaposition of the insignificance of the mailman and the shocking news he is to deliver, is suggestive of the strong dramatic tendency in the poet's final comment, "Here comes the receiver's horrendous hour." In life, shocking news is not preceded by ill omens. On the contrary, it can arrive as simply as with a knock at the door, or a note slipped under it.

The identity of the mailman is an elaborate metaphor, a clue which leads to further explication of meanings behind the scene. For example, the identity of the mailman is associated with the message he delivers, while the message is associated with the bad news a person receives. To start with association and end with the formation of associated objects in a conceit is a main characteristic of Feng Chih's early lyricism. Another example can be found in the poem "A Starry Sky," which is indicative of Feng's poetic style in his first poetry volume, *Songs of Yesterday*:

Into my bosom,
I gather all the stars;
With threads of love,
I string them up
like drops of tear pearls;
And have them woven into an overcoat
to put on my lover.
With the crescent moon
I slowly take down
from the west,
I comb her soft tender hair.

Playing the flute and the pipe,
our music harmonized;
We sing to the classic immortals,
We fly to the end of the sky,
and spread out an overcoat
to rearrange the star pattern in the sky.
Playing our duet again,
we transcend all worldly glories
and shallow grievances.[6]

A few years later, poems like "I Am a Small River," "Fig" and "Snake" were constructed with romantic images to form plausible conceits, especially in "I Am a Small River,"

I am a small river,
flowing inadvertently beside you;
You casually cast your roseate shadows
into my soft, gentle ripplings.

I pass through a forest,
Ripples widely drifting,
Tailoring the green leaves' shadows
to a dress of yours.

I pass through a flowery bush,
Ripples softly shimmering,
Weaving the colored flower shadows
Into a florid coronet of yours.

I finally enter
into the cruel ocean;
Winds high, waves rough,
They break the florid coronet,
and smash the dress.

Endlessly I follow the sea tides drifting.
Your roseate shadow
vanishes like the colorful sea clouds.[7]

The inner experience of the poet is the flow of a small river, while the outer experience—his lover's shadow—is projected on the river until they merge. In the constant movement of the river, past experiences disintegrate and new ones become integrated to form a richer memory—the final flow to the ocean. The desire to create verisimilitude of action drove the poet to explore various literary models, and the ideal model adopted eventually by Feng Chih was the lyric-narrative.

In 1923, when Feng Chih had just graduated from high school and matriculated at Peking University, he returned to Cho-hsien, his hometown in Hopei province, for the spring vacation. During his stay there, he wrote a series of sixteen narrative lyrics entitled "Returning Home," in which the young poet, torn by his memories of the past and frustrations of the present, tried to convey his feelings. Although "Returning Home" was completed in early 1923, it was not until 1929 that a few poems from this series appeared in the journal *Creation Quarterly*. At that time, the poet's first poetry collection, *Songs of Yesterday*, had been in print for two years, and his long lyric-narrative poems "Drapery" and "The Silkworm Stallion" had received wide applause and public recognition. Compared to the warm reception accorded to these poems, "Returning Home" seemed to be deprived of the plaudits it deserved.

Two related terms have been proposed here, namely, the narrative lyric and the lyric-narrative. The former is basically concerned with individual response to experience, through which reality is perceived and then narrated with a high degree of subjectivity. The latter is objective and impersonal, and its events are not basically concerned with the poet's personal experience, they instead derive from folk lyrics and from the oral tradition which usually assume the form of a myth or a tale tinged with local color. Nevertheless, there is a strong lyric touch on the poet's part, adding to the narrative treatment, so that a subjective, lyrical perspective is fused with an objective narration of events. Consequently, the lyric dimension increases as the narrative color intensifies.

"Returning Home" belongs to the category of the narrative lyric, and in it the poet uses dissimilar objects to express his personal feelings. Various kinds of objects are juxtaposed so as to evoke a chain reaction in the poet's emotions, and they also serve as objective correlatives which mainly reflect the subjective feelings of the narrator. In the "Proem," Feng Chih expresses his attitude toward returning as:

> Ordinary flowers bloom in my hometown,
> No extraordinary fruits of marvel.
> Since I have no place to stay,
> I can only return, temporarily.[8]

The theme of the entire poem is stated in these lines. The poet knows his reason for returning: "Since I have no place to stay." He returns reluctantly to a place where there are only ordinary flowers. Nevertheless, the frustration simultaneously suggests a basic quest of the singer—to start a new journey and search for utopian dwelling. However, reality holds him back; he is instead returning to a negative world where flowers produce no marvellous fruits. The objects he relates and the events he narrates, then, are only reflections of a frustrated mind. Such are the characteristics of Feng Chih's early narrative lyrics.

"Flower" and "A Bright Pearl" are the second and third poems in the series; both present external defeats and a state of restlessness in the poet's mind. "Flower" consists of four stanzas, each standing for a stage of experience. The poet pities the flower because:

> It bears
> a bud in half-bloom,
> knows not the beauty of itself.
> Its profound meaning is contained
> only in the spring sun.
>
> All around it
> are bramble bushes;
> Who are its sisters among them?
>
> Softly will the feeble petals stretch,
> Gradually will they disappear.
>
> Being ignorant of the beauty
> of its blooming and budding,
> it chooses the yellow flowery briars
> to become its sisters.
> Finally it withers with tears,
> Without knowing its ill fortune.[9]

Through metaphor of the flower, we see the transcience of human life. However, the most regrettable event, according to the poet, is to have neglected youth and to have spent life unheeded, as if it were only a common flower in the brambles. Thus, the flower's fate is the symbolic destiny the poet tries to avoid, and his narrative of the flower becomes the lyric expression of his personal perceptions.

The metaphor continues in "A Bright Pearl," which reflects the inner anxiety of the intellect. The conflict of possessing the pearl is like that of returning home:

> I have a bright pearl
> hidden deeply inside of me;
> For the fear of overexposing its lustre,
> I wrap it with my tear membranes.
>
> My bright pearl is
> what is left from ransacking;
> Its greenish lustre
> illuminates only my grievances.[10]

Despite all the adversities, the attitude in the series remains
optimistic and unyielding. The fourth poem, "In This Mean World,"
expresses this outlook in asking "In this mean world/ I dare not ask
for anything./ But if my greatest hope/ does not lie in this world,/
Where is it then?"[11] The conflict engendered by remaining in a
world of suffering, and dreading the terrifying experience of this
suffering is further seen in a poem written in Peking a year later
(1924). "On Top Of The Pleasant-View Pavilion" reveals a patriotic
bafflement:

> A heavenly world!
> This is the sorrow of
> the last emperor of T'ang.
> I look everywhere,
> Moods in low key,
> But if I descend,
> How shall I go down?
>
> Heaven is silent,
> World is clamorous;
> How can I stay here lingering?
> Lonesome and remorseful,
> Where shall I return?
>
> Clouds sadden,
> Water wrinkles;
> If I know their profundities,
> I would plunge into the river,
> Or escape to the West Mountain,
> Deep into the clouds.
>
> I tremble and shiver,
> Oh, wind, how shall I fly down?
> In an opened book,
> I found a yellow flower
> pressed in the pages.
> For my fate, I kiss it,
> For its fate, I weep.[12]

Feng Chih previously affirmed that his greatest hope, indeed, lay
in this world, and therefore, neither could the last emperor's es-
capist desire become a reality, nor could plunging into the dark
realm of death settle the poet's bewilderment. The inability to comprehend other meanings of things or events ("If I know their pro-

fundities") hints at the intellectual dilemma of being unable to communicate with the world. In the fifteenth poem of this series, a beggar intrudes as a symbol of such alienation:

> I am really hungry now.
> I walk on the road,
> Sing a song here and there,
> But still hungry.
>
> There is a girl by the door,
> I cannot help it,
> And I beg for something to eat;
> She takes out a coin in her hand,
>
> I say, lady, money cannot help,
> Please give me the rice you've made,
> Or what is left over,
> For me to eat.
>
> As I am making the request,
> A harsh crone comes out,
> Quietly the girl goes in;
> I continue on my journey,
> Twice hungry.[13]

Two months after Feng Chih completed "Returning Home," he began to incorporate folklore and mythical legends into his lyrics. These poems resulted in a series of lyric-narratives unequalled at the time. "The Flutist" was written in 1923, "Drapery" in 1924 and "The Silkworm Stallion" in 1925; all are love tragedies. "The Flutist" is the least known of the three, perhaps because of the popularity and extensive anthologizing of the other two. It tells of a young flutist who secludes himself in the mountains for many years. One night when he is alone and playing the flute, his heart responds to a mirage of a maiden harmonizing with him. The next day, he leaves the mountain, searches for and finds her. They fall in love, but the girl's parents are reluctant to give their daughter away to a stranger. The girl becomes seriously ill. The anxious flutist dreams that his flute tells him that the flute spirit can cure the girl's illness. He awakes and breaks the flute in order to make medicine for his love. The girl, consequently, recovers and the parents consent to their marriage. However, although they deeply love each other, the flutist is unhappy because of the loss of his flute. As a result, he then becomes seriously ill and now the girl has to break her flute to save her husband. Finally, the sorrow of losing both their beloved flutes, or rather, music and poetry, drives the two lovers to disappear into the deep mountains.

There are convictions held by the poet which lie beneath the surface of this love story. First, he believes in the poetic form as best expressing the supreme fiction of human life in which the making of music is vital in sustaining the flutist's seclusion from the world. Second, an escape to art is a way to reject the mundane world because, according to Feng Chih, the human world and the art world are antithetical, as when he describes the flutist leaving his seclusion to search for his ideal beauty: "Next morning/ he is at a loss/ Playing his flute and holding his gown,/ he runs toward the turbulent world."[14]

There is also a close relationship, both in theme and in the attitude of the poet who views society as hostile to the kinship of humanity, between "The Flutist" and "Returning Home." In the latter, the poet expresses his frustration by asking where besides in this world would his greatest hope lie? The flutist, on the other hand, perceives that the world is turbulent and yet he has to emerge from his seclusion and submerge himself in the turbulence because of his quest for the harmonizer (a symbol for the appreciative audience.) The search, therefore, is a heroic event, an adventure taken with the concept of suffering. Although the process is painful, it can also be viewed as a means of acquiring higher knowledge through the breaking of individual art forms (the flutes). The return is a final mutual understanding between art and the reception of art. In conclusion, the poet implores his audience, "Please don't be sad,/ For they have returned to the mountains/ A happy ending, so to speak."[15]

The nunnery in "Drapery," like the mountains in "The Flutist," is looked upon as a retreat from the troublesome world. In contrast to the "turmoils" aroused in this world, the nunnery is described as quiet and static, "neither stale, nor fresh." The cause for the young nun to take her vows is a weak outcry against the traditional Chinese prearranged marriage: "I just happen to hear someone say—/ the one who is going to share my life/ will be an ugly idiot."[16] The image of the nunnery expresses a deliberate alienation from the mundane world in search of utopia, and a purgatorial redemption from sins one has committed in this life, or in previous and later ones. In this poem, however, the irony of fate continues to haunt the young nun. After she deliberately evades marrying the man she does not love, and secludes herself in the nunnery, she is, in turn, forbidden by the sacred orders to express her love to a passing shepherd, whose music has rekindled the passions of love within her.

In Feng Chih's lyric-narratives, there are three consistent motifs: the vagabond, equivalent to the heroic adventurer in ancient Chinese mythical legends; the music, or the artist's expression; and the artifact, or the subject of metaphysical union. The vagabond usually bears either the status of a homeless wanderer drifting purposelessly, or that of a traveller with a firm destination. The entrance and departure of these figures bound the dream world of Feng Chih's narratives. For example, the unattached wandering of the shepherd in "Drapery" contrasts with the determined hermit in "The Flutist" who clutches his flute, vowing to search out his love in this world. On the other hand, the purposeless, carefree passing of the shepherd is only the daily routine of bringing his cattle to graze; this is the occasion of his being attracted to the young nun. In other words, herding his cattle is his primary motive, while playing his flute is only a secondary act which has no overt purpose of attracting the nun in the nunnery. In her despair over the impossibility of union with the shepherd, the nun starts to weave a drapery, an artifact which turns the music of the shepherd into the woven images of her mind. Like the challenge of language to the poet's imagery, the making of the tapestry is a device to crystallize the maker's craftsmanship. The artifact itself is a romantic mirror reflecting the combination of imagination and reality by which the poet strives to reconcile himself with the outside world.

"The Silkworm Stallion" also hints at the poet's conflicting feelings and persisting hope for reconciliation. The poem consists of three sections, each preceded by a lyric episode which successfully controls the pace as well as the changing of the narrative views. Linking these episodes together is the legend of the silkworm stallion, which appears as one of the mythical tales in the classic *Soushen Chi*. Feng Chih footnoted the poem by giving a summary of the tale as follows:

It was told that once the father of a maid who tended silkworms was kidnapped; only his horse remained. The maid's mother vowed that whoever brought her husband back would have the hand of her daughter. Upon hearing this, the horse broke loose of the halter and galloped away. A few days later, it brought back the maid's father. The woman then revealed her promise to her husband who rejected the idea. The horse neighed vehemently and was slaughtered. Its hide was exposed in the courtyard. Suddenly, the hide infolded the maid and disappeared. Later, she was found bundled in a mulberry bush. The maid had already been transformed into a silkworm.[17]

Like the nun in "Drapery," the stallion suffers from the delusion that under the pretext of love and trust, illusion can turn into reality and the normal ways can be discarded. Feng Chih also hints that death and transformation can serve to reverse the situation. The ending is gothic, but within its haunting effects, the poem has successfully fused the tale with the three sections of lyrical episodes in which the romantic spirit has strengthened the narrator's apparent sympathy for the stallion. Behind the objective view and seemingly impersonal narration of the tale, by inserting lyrical episodes the poet has found a way to transform the mode of narration. The tale no longer exists in the way it was first written, nor in the prosaic narration of other story tellers, but now possesses an independent style of its own, an expression that is unique to the poet and to his own time.

CHAPTER 5

The Later Search for the Folk Lyric

T HE literary policy regarding proletarian literature in China was basically established when Mao Tse-tung presented his "Talks at the Yenan Forum on Literature and Art" in 1942. The guidelines Mao expressed were designed for leftist writers whose ideological beliefs and literary practices were deemed incongruous. Strictly speaking, Mao's views can hardly be regarded as literary aesthetics due to their political, sociological and revolutionary content. Yet they thoroughly determined the role of the writer in the socialist endeavor. The personal artistry of the writer was no longer esteemed by the audience as the criterion for artistic achievment. Instead, it was considered time for the writer to turn away from his individuality and to begin serving the masses, comprising basically the peasants, workers and soldiers.

Poets like Feng Chih and Ai Ch'ing, who were still working under heavy European influence, reacted in ways which opened a new phase of modern Chinese poetry. How were they to adjust to such a change? Ai Ch'ing's reaction was a vigorous one. He demanded that his audience should try to "understand" and to "respect" writers in return.[1] Feng Chih's reaction was quite different in that he neither dissented nor fell silent. Instead, he modestly began to study in order to adapt himself to the social as well as literary changes then occuring in China. It is true that after 1949 he was not as productive as before. This temporary silence, however, was probably due to his taking the time to learn a new approach and to experiment rather than to any rejection of change as such.

Apparently, Feng Chih was under critical attack during the year 1957.[2] In that year he published a collection of poems called *Hsi-chiao Chi*, or *Collection of the West Suburb*, in Peking. Feng defended himself in his "Afterword" to the album by saying that be-

67

cause of the venomous attacks he had received, "I decided to pub-
lish this album as my reply. My poems are few, but I wish to repeat
that it was only after the liberation of the country and the founding
of the People's Republic of China that I actually began writing
poetry again. This shows that New China has not 'frozen' my
creativity, but has, on the contrary, thawed my stagnation like a
spring breeze."[3] He went on to explain that he was conscious of the
fact that his present poems might appear "crude and superficial,"
but that he firmly believed that he was "on the right track" when he
compared his new work with the poems he had written before the
Liberation.[4] From this statement we can understand that Feng's
decrease in production was due to his preparation, to his seeking out
"the right track," which is not a personal path but "a road entirely
for the masses." Regarding the elevation and popularization of art,
the poet bluntly states that "if the poet does not sing for the benefit
of the masses, then no matter how wonderful his feelings or how
ingenious his metaphors, he is only wasting his time and energy."[5]

If the poet's functions are to serve the masses and, at the same
time, to try to elevate his materials and to give them a higher artistic
value, then where and how could he find his source of imagination?
In 1958, a year after Mao Tse-tung revealed his classical poems to
the public, the country was feverishly exploring what modes of expression were typical of the intellectual reflection of the masses. The
editorial section of the "People's Daily" advised people to dig deep
into the great earth of poetry, and to let ballads, mountain songs and
narrative poems come gushing out of the ground like crude oil.[6] To
fulfill his role, the poet at the same time had "to be submerged in
the masses and to unite with the masses, to learn from the masses
and from the songs created by the masses."[7] The result of learning
from the masses and the simultaneous leading of the masses to a
higher realm of imagination was a union of Revolutionary Realism
and Revolutionary Romanticism. Chou Yang, in his "New Ballads
Pioneer the New Road of Poetry," agreed that there was an imminent need for this realistic-romantic spirit if the creative techniques
of Socialist Realism were to be utilized[8]. Feng Chih, on the other
hand, saw the balladic mode as the most appropriate vehicle of
expression, and particularly in reference to his personal creativity,
the balladic narration as the most appropriate continuation to his
lyric-narratives following the abandonment of his personal mysticism. Feng realized that it was these ballads that caught the real

feelings of the new socialist era and that reflected the magnanimous spirit of the people of New China. The ballad writer "combats nature with hard labor," and he is "optimistic, confident, and has no consideration for his personal self."[9]

Since personal value is rejected and instead mass values are emphasized, there naturally is a great change in the profile of the hero. Personal heroics, or individual agonies in ivory towers, are rejected as being only a reflection of a very narrow view of life, too impotent to express the existing ideology of Socialist Realism. Feng Chih defines the new role of the poet, the role in which the poet must understand the masses and finally become one with them:

For time present, the poet should be a singer. For time future, he should be a prophet. But if he doesn't thoroughly understand the life of the present, his prophecy will be abstract and empty. If he can't see the broad prospects of the future, his present songs will be too limited and stagnant.[10]

The above statement marks the end of Feng Chih's pre-1949 career as a sonneteer and the beginning of his career as a people's balladeer. The difference between the new ballads and the old ones lies in the "projected image of the commoners becoming their own masters . . . , the audacity to throw away their old burdens . . . and the belief and confidence in one's ability to conquer difficulties and to no longer be a slave to nature, but to master nature and to command nature."[11] Feng Chih finally leaves his once preferred "solitude" and throws himself into a world of vitality and promises, into a society in which the hero no longer needs to be nobly born or supernaturally endowed to perform his heroic tasks. In the ten-year period from 1949 to 1959, Feng Chih began to portray characters who were to be found among the masses, who possessed common characteristics in the way in which they served the course of socialism and whose heroics derived not from the presentation of their personal glories, but in the way in which they challenged nature in order to better society. A poem entitled "To P'an Ch'ang-yu" describes a common factory worker named P'an Ch'ang-yu who has become a modern Prometheus:

> No one heard of such a thing in the past,
> Fire still burning, but the furnace is repaired.
> You love your work, keep up the production,
> Receive guidance from foreign instructors.

Building a fire wall inside the furnace,
Flames hardening steel still ablaze.
When the repair work is about done,
Suddenly the fire wall collapsing.

You put on a water-soaked cotton coat.
Jumping into the furnace of six hundrèd degrees in
  temperature,
You lead everyone to the repair in turns,
Piling up the fire wall again.

This old story three years ago
Caused a sensation in all factories, large and small;
Now the furnace no longer requires frequent repairs
Because this event has set a good example.

We want to maintain peace,
With a devotion like yours.
We are ready all the time
To jump into the high-heated furnace.[12]

This poem is one of many songs describing the booming steel indus-
try that was developing during the early 1950s in China. It has four
layers of meaning. First, unlike the old ballads, this poem, as a new
song, is "no longer a reflection of the painful, exploited lives of the
labor class, nor is it a reflection of the self-sufficient bourgeoisie and
their customs and psychology."[13] It portrays instead the unyielding
spirit of the working class, which now confidently works as a group
to fight and conquer its environmental obstacles. Second, the purpose of P'an Ch'ang-yu's adventure is genuine and socially com-
mendable because he is not taking his risk for personal glory, but for
the benefit of the masses, and for the socialist ideal which is inextricably tied to the fate of the Chinese people. Thirdly, P'an
Ch'ang-yu's action is creative and antitraditional ("No one heard of
such a thing in the past,/ Fire still burning, but the furnace is
repaired"). Only by such unprecedented and revolutionary concepts
can the old, corrupt China be changed into a new and energetic
nation. Finally, the poem implies that if one wishes to attain his
purposes, which ought to be, generally speaking, for the benefit of
the majority, then one must be prepared to sacrifice oneself in every
possible way, despite all dangers and adversities. Feng Chih implies
that we should be able to sacrifice ourselves at any time for the sake
of maintaining peace ("To jump into the high-heated furnace").

The deep concern, as we have now seen in Feng Chih's poetry, is no longer with the intellectual agony of the mind, but with bold and selfless action. In another poem, "Old Hero Meng T'ai," the poet illustrates his ideas with the example of an old factory worker who, despite his illness, saves a high-temperature furnace from explosion. The action of the poem takes place "one winter" when the old man "was staying in a convalescent home." The furnace had something go wrong with it at midnight, and was about to explode, when:

> Forgetting the night, the illness,
> And the long distance of the road,
> You threw yourself into the thick mist.
> Risking your life, you saved the furnace.[14]

This kind of heroic theme, as we see from the narratives of P'an Ch'ang-yu and Meng T'ai, is quite different from the themes of Feng Chih's previous narrative lyrics. Such a poem shows how Feng Chih has broadened his lyric spectrum from the personal to the social. What he feels, in contrast to his viewpoint in his earlier days, is not only his personal reaction, but also a reflection of the group consciousness. Regal heroics are highly discriminative, but a people's hero is universal, in that he acts for the good of all. The people's hero acts out of revolutionary ideals with devotion and self-sacrifice, and without privileges. He is willing to do anything for the sake of justice and the people. Unlike the frail characters compared to small insects or feeble plants in Feng's early sonnets, the heroes in these new poems no longer depend upon the mercy of nature, but challenge nature. They are like the young technicians in "Surveyors," of whom Feng Chih says, "Nature has lost completely its mysteries/ before their attentions."[15]

Feng now believes in a liberated China in which everyone is his or her own master. This particularly includes those people whose social status was once negligible, held down by exploiters. One poem confirming this belief in the possibility of people's transformation is "Han Po The Woodcutter." Han Po is a virtual nonentity in the old society, submitting docilely to his cruel fate. As the poet once wrote in an early sonnet, life "conceives/ Only the whirling wind, the coming of a comet."[16] Han Po is first seen leading the wretched life of a woodcutter:

> He chopped wood all his life
> So his landlord could cook and eat;
> He chopped wood all his life
> So his landlord could get warm by the fire.
>
> But he himself never
> Ate or wore enough;
> No matter how foul the weather was
> He chopped his wood incessantly.[17]

Finally, in a heavy storm Han Po is frozen to death. Too weak actually to seek revenge, his spirit can only slip out and bitterly continue cutting wood. Han Po stands as a symbol for the thousands of persecuted Chinese who died nameless deaths:

> So many Han Po in the past
> Died of cold and hunger.
> Our sympathies could only be expressed
> With the moonlight at midnight.[18]

The moonlight here not only suggests the fading of brightness and the invasion of darkness, but also is a gesture of tragic lyricism which, unlike the fair sunlight of justice, is incapable of sufficient pity and sympathy. Feng Chih bids a final farewell to this very personal lament with an unabashed outcry:

> Tomorrow we will struggle
> Against the landlords
> And purge them.
> No longer will Han Po feel ashamed
> To appear in broad daylight.[19]

Witnessing the solid achievements of a new China, Feng Chih's disillusionment with his egotistic past is understandable. However, in depicting the remarkable progress of his country, Feng stumbles into a stylistic dilemma in which the poet's thinking has to conform to public consciousness. The point of view taken in his work is no longer a personal one, but is instead more nearly the point of view taken by the masses. The poet is expected to articulate the collective voice of the people. This sets up a new and difficult barrier for the contemplative lyricist who has spent most of his life in mastering the use of dynamic imagery and metaphors in order to convey the com-

plexity of his meanings. The prevailing style of the people's literature is one which is direct, realistic and simple. It is not that the
poet is unable to mobilize his own ideas and words, but rather that
his expression is greatly hampered by the nature of the themes he
adopts, and by the requirement that he conform to the common
ideology and slogans. In other words, Feng Chih has broken out of
the small cage of personal lyricism and entered a larger cage of
common ideology. Examples of this are numerous in Feng Chih's
later poems. Take, for instance, a poem called "A National Day
Parade":

> Colorful flowers, at T'ien-an Gate, held high,
> Balloons, at T'ien-an Gate, floating;
> Deep inside, everyone feels
> Chairman Mao is smiling at him.
>
> Our parade is happiness,
> Our parade is peace;
> All over the world our slogans
> Echo.
>
> A thousand cheers at T'ien-an Gate,
> Doves fluttering;
> Deep inside, everyone feels
> Chairman Mao is waving to him.
>
> Our troop is diligent,
> Our troop is constructive;
> Our mission is for the
> Benefit of the world's laborers.
>
> Records of success, at T'ien-an Gate, held high,
> Red flags, at T'ien-an Gate, floating;
> Everyone feels in his heart
> Chairman Mao is warmly guiding him.[20]

Rather than being discouraged, Feng Chih finds that to follow the
will of the masses is not only positive but a promising course for the
future of modern Chinese poetry. He firmly believes that the new
ballad forms are the products of voices which speak directly from
the thoughts and activities of the masses. He points out:

"these thoughts and activities, of course, can also be reflected in the new
poetry. However, since the new ballad is created directly out of popular

labor, what it reflects is more vivid and touching. There are poems in the new poetry that are produced directly out of labor, but most of them spring from observation and contemplation. The new poetry is no match for the new ballads, either in form or in content."[21]

This preference for the new ballad instead of the poetry forms of the pre-1949 era is suggestive of Feng Chih's own struggle to find a vehicle which will provide not only the freedom of poetic, imaginative creativity but also a realistic portrayal of the life of the masses. Feng continues:

Now, many fine ballads are blooming in thousands of colors. Many comrades have illustrated many of them in their critical essays on ballads. There is only one ballad I would like to mention here. It was written by a sixteen-year old girl named Lu Chin-chih. (See "People's Daily," December 16, 1958, p. 6):

> The kindness of the Communist Party
> is long and long.
> I don't know which one to sing about.
> Like thousands of fresh flowers,
> All red and fragrant.

What a wonderful poem! I have nothing but praise for this poem. Firstly, it makes people feel the unrelenting kindness the Communist Party has shown to the laborers. Secondly, the author uses the red and fragrant flowers to make a comparison to the indecision of our minds in trying to choose which kindness of the Party to praise. At the same time, the impression is conveyed that everything in our society is perfect and lovable. Thirdly, the tone is very natural. Although "Communist Party" is a tri-syllabic word, the extra syllable is free from the "seven-syllable" pattern. Finally, although the third and fourth lines may be a common metaphor in rural areas, nevertheless, adopting them here as a comparison to the kindness of the Communist Party is a golden touch, a powerful expression.[22]

This poem, in fact, is not as wonderful as Feng Chih claims. First, the beginning two lines are incompatible. If the kindness is described as "long and long," then it is a qualitative measure. However, the author says "I don't know which one to sing about," apparently referring to it as a quantitative measure. Second, if the comparison in the first couplet is not apt, how can we compare the thousand flowers (quantitative) with the unrelenting kindness (qualitative) of the Communist Party? Third, we can see that the so-called "new ballad" is in a crude stage of development, still to be perfected by such legitimate artists as Feng Chih, who can supply a golden touch to simple metaphors:

> Deeply the Party's roots are planted in
> man's heart,
> And they have reached six million hearts.
> Oh, the unreachable mountain is not as high
> as the Party's fame,
> Oh, the fathomless sea is not as deep
> as the Party's wisdom.[23]

What then are the potentials of the new ballad that can take the place of the new poetry? Feng Chih lays out his prospect as follows:

The subject matter expressed in these new ballads is so broad and refreshing that it is more touching and maneuverable than the subject matter in the new poetry. This can be explained in that the form of the new ballad is not fixed, but is active and lively; not to mention that the liberated ideas of the laboring class have shown an incomparable power during the Great Leap Forward. Even high mountains and great rivers cannot stop their ambitious projects. When they wish to sing about their ideas and feelings, how can they be bound by the limitations of any poetic form?[24]

Instead of viewing this passage as proving the merits of the new ballad, one can rather view it as proof of its weakness. Phrases such as "the liberated ideas of the laboring class have shown an incomparable power," or "Even high mountains and great rivers cannot stop their ambitious projects" are typical examples of hyperbole. Once a literary content is exaggerated, the author draws himself still further away from solid facts. The unrealistic presentation of these facts leads to unrealistic assumptions, which are often expressed under the disguise of hyperbole:

> In our country
> Difficulties forever surrender to us:
> Victory is the project of moving mountains
> and seas,
> Victory is the thought of conquering difficulties,
> Victory is the day which equals twenty years,
> Victory is the ever-revolutionary Communist Party.[25]

What we see here is mere dogmatism, an unconvincing shouting of slogans. If such a style does project the future of the people's poetry, then poetry will be limited to its avowed purpose of popularization rather than achieving the elevation of artistry.

In 1973, roughly sixteen years after the emergence of the new ballads, Hsu Kai-yu, a professor of Chinese and Comparative Literature at San Francisco State University, visited Peking and conversed with Feng Chih for three hours. Nothing much was revealed in this meeting. Hsu avoided touching directly upon the literary aftermath of the Cultural Revolution, which had somehow aborted the growth of Chinese ballads. Instead he asked about Feng Chih's personal experiences during the literary controversies. Feng Chih's response was phrased elegantly, but, Hsu reports, "He was not nearly as generous with his words in answering my questions as he was with his smile."[26]

What is Feng Chih now writing? Hsu reports that Feng occasionally writes in the traditional lines of five and seven syllables, possibly a result of his extensive studies of Tu Fu and Lu Yu. Perhaps Feng Chih is taking a retrospective view of the new ballads. This may be the result of the publication of Mao Tse-tung's classical poems. Will these traditional five and seven syllable lines serve as a new inspiration to revivify Feng's creativity? Or rather, will the classical mode, with its highly compressed and condensed patterns, be more suited to Feng Chih's personal inclinations? We have already seen that when Feng Chih falls silent, it indicates that he is eagerly searching for a new approach. Thus we wait optimistically, anticipating another meaningful change to complete Feng Chih's splendid poetic career.

Translation of The Sonnets

Translator's note:

The following text of Feng Chih's sonnets has been translated from the second edition of *The Sonnets* published in Shanghai, 1949. The first edition, published in Kweilin in 1942, appeared without either a preface or an afterword.

Preface

In 1941, I was living on a mountain near Kunming and had to go into the city twice a week. It was a trip of about fifteen miles, and walking back and forth was pleasant exercise. A person alone on mountain paths and meadows cannot help but look around him and ruminate. At that particular point in my life, it seemed as if I saw a great deal more and thought more exuberantly than usual. I had not, in the years between 1931 and 1940, written much poetry: I had penned no more than a score of poems.

Once, on a winter afternoon, when I was looking at a few silvery airplanes, blue like crystals, hovering in the azure sky, I was reminded of the "roc dream" of the ancients. Following the rhythms of my footsteps, I casually composed a rhymed poem. When I got home, I wrote the poem down and found, quite accidentally, that it was a sonnet. The poem composed that afternoon is the eighth sonnet in this collection, and it is somewhat unnatural in that it emerged after a particularly barren spell in my creativity.

The circumstance surrounding the composing of this poem are incidental, but I had, for some time, been burdened with the weight of my past experiences. There were experiences which kept recurring in my mind, and people who, in one way or another, had sustained me in the past. Too, there were encounters with natural phenomena which had provided apocalyptic moments. Could I not then leave a gesture of gratitude to all this? I decided then to write a poem for each object that had touched my life: from the eternal souls in history to the nameless country children and farmers' wives, from the historically important city far away to the insects and grasses on a nearby slope, and from a personal slice of life to the experiences shared by all people.

I sometimes wrote two or three poems a day, but on other occasions I stopped midway and left a poem unfinished for a period of time before returning to it. In this way, I managed to compose a total of twenty-seven poems before autumn came and I became seriously ill.

When I recovered, I felt that I had nothing left except my enfeebled body, but as I regained my strength I began working on the revisions of the twenty-seven poems. While working on the revisions, I seemed to experience a sense of release, as if a weight of responsibility was being lifted from me.

I have been asked why I have employed the sonnet form for my compositions, and I am afraid I really have no idea, except to say that the structure and rhythms associated with this form provided a natural framework for the ideas I wished to convey. In the words of Mr. Li Kuang-t'ien, "because it rises and falls layer after layer, concentrates gradually and dissolves . . . variates and conforms [as] its rhymes interweave," the form suited me perfectly. But the conscious intention of transplanting this essentially Western form to China never really occurred to me.

It has been seven years since I composed the sonnets. The sky over Peiping is as azure and crystalline as it was in Kunming. There are silvery planes seen frequently in the sky, but facing them now I no longer think of the "roc dream" of the ancients. The only things which strike my mind these days are the numerous catastrophes on earth. When I happen to see new born puppies, I tend, in the grip of passion, to say, "you'll bark and bring forth light in the dark of night," and to a complicated and deceitful society, "give my strait heart a vast universe."

A collection of poems is very much like a piece of sculpture or a painting. It should exist on its own terms with no need of explanation. When the first edition of these poems was published in 1942 in Kweilin by the Tomorrow Society, it appeared without either a preface or an afterword. But with this, the second edition, I have felt the necessity to express the thoughts written above.

February 5, 1948
Peiping

Sonnet One

We are ready to receive profoundly,
Unexpected mysteries,
In these prolix times; the sudden appearance
of a comet, the whirling, gusty wind:

At this very moment, our lives
Are in the first embrace,
Joys and sorrows come quickly to our eyes
Solidifying into towering forms.

We praise tiny insects
Braving the conjugation;
Resisting imminent danger,

Their wondrous lives brought to an end.
Our sole lives conceive
The whirling wind, the coming of a comet.

Sonnet Two

What falls from our bodies
We allow to turn into dust:
We align ourselves in time like
autumn trees, each

Offering leaves and belated blossoms
to the autumn wind, that our
trunks may stretch into frigid winters;
We align ourselves with nature: molted cicada

Leaving its discarded skin in soil and mud;
We arrange ourselves for that
Coming death, a passage of the song,

Falling from the corpus of music
And only the body remains,
Transformed, a series of silent mountains.

Sonnet Three

You, soughing jade tree in the autumn wind,
Build a solemn temple of music
in my ears; let me
Enter reverently.

You, again, sky-piercing tower,
Rising, like the body
of a saint before me,
Sanctify a clamorous city.

You, constantly shedding your bark,
I see you rise 'midst the withering season.
From intersecting meadow paths

I turn to you, my guide, and say
"Long live forever," that I, by inches,
Wish to rot in earth, covered by your roots.

Sonnet Four

Often, when I think of life
I want to pray before you;
You, a bunch of pale grass
Have not failed your name.

But you exist apart from all names,
Live a minute life,
Never fail dignity and purity,
then quietly complete your life and death.

All description, all tumult
Comes close to you; some wither,
Others join your quietude.

Your great pride
Is achieved in your denial.
I pray before you, for life.

Sonnet Five

I shall never forget
That water city of the West,
Symbol of the human world,
Conglomerate of a thousand lonelinesses.

Each an island,
Each seeking a friend in another.
Your hand touches mine,
A bridge across the water.

You smile at me,
A window opens
From an island on the other side.

In the deep and silent night,
Windows close
And bridges empty.

Sonnet Six

I often see in the plain
A country lad, a farmer's wife
Crying to a silent sky,
A certain punishment perhaps,

A broken toy,
A husband's death,
The illness of a son.
Incessant crying,

All life framed;
And outside,
No life, no world.

I feel their tears,
Flowing since ancient times
For a hopeless universe.

Sonnet Seven

Under a warm sun
We come to the country,
Meandering rivers
Drawn into a great sea.

The same awakening
in our hearts,
A similar fate
upon our shoulders.

A common god
who worries over us;
Till the danger passes,

Diverging streets
Again absorb us:
Sea scattering into rivers.

Sonnet Eight

It is an ancient dream from the past
And now there's this disordered world,
I wish to fly on a roc
and chat with the peaceful stars.

A thousand-year-old dream, like an aged man,
Anticipates only the best progeny,
Now, someone flies to the stars
But doesn't forget the disordered world.

They want to learn
How to circulate and to haul in
The stellate order of this world,

And like a flash, they plunge into the void.
Now the old dream's a meteor
lying in some deserted mountain, far from the sea.

Sonnet Nine

All these years you grow between life and death,
Once you return to this degraded city,
Listen to the foolish songs in town,
You would feel like a classic hero

Returning after a thousand years,
From the changing of this disgraced children
He will find no gesture of the glorious days,
He will be shocked, dizzy.

On the battlefield, an immortal hero;
In the open sky, finally
an aimless kite.

But don't complain of your fate;
you have surpassed them, they could no longer
tie up your soaring, your far-reaching.

Sonnet Ten

Your name, often put among
many other names, makes
no difference; but you have
forever sustained your own lustre;

Only at the passage of dawn and dusk
Could you be recognized—the brightest star;
At midnight, you make no difference
Among other stars; so many youths

Obtain their proper lives
From your calm apocalypse. Now that you're dead,
We deeply feel you can no longer

participate in our future tasks—
If this world resuscitates
And things straighten out.

Sonnet Eleven

Once, many years ago of an evening,
You felt an awakening for a few youths;
You have felt countless disillusionments
But that vision has never faded.

I hold you in affection and gratitude, and will
always turn to you for the sake of our age.
It has been destroyed by some who are fools,
Its protector was, throughout his life,

rejected by this world.
You caught a glimpse of light a few times,
But as you turn your head, our era is covered by dark clouds.

You have completed your journey, risking
the hardships, only the grass along the sidewalks
provokes you to hopeful smiles.

Sonnet Twelve

You endured starvation in a deserted village,
Thought about the dead filling up the trenches,

But you sang the elegies incessantly
for the fall of human magnificence.

Warriors die, were wounded on battlefields,
Meteors fell at sky's end,
Ten thousand horses disappeared with the floating clouds
and your life was the sacrifice for them.

Your poverty shone,
The tattered robes of a saint.
A single thread from it

An inexhaustable spiritual force in this world
All kingdoms before your brilliance
Are only reflections of pitiful images.

Sonnet Thirteen

You were born into a family of commoners,
shed tears for many ordinary girls.
You feared, revered the one who rules the realm
and lived a life of eighty tranquil years.

Just as the globe turns silently
without a minute or a second's rest
New signs evolve, all the time, everywhere.
In wind and rain, fair weather and foul,

Comes new health from heavy sickness,
New strength out of desperate love;
You know why moths plunge into fire,

Why snakes shed their skins in growth;
All things observe your creed
which reveals the meaning of life: Death and metamorphosis.

Sonnet Fourteen

Your passion, with every turn
inflames: a sheaf of sunflower,
Dark, languorous cypresses,
People walking

Beneath the scorching sun, they too,
inflamed, plead on high;
But a small, withered tree
in the early spring, a tiny prison yard,

A woman peeling potatoes in a darkened room,
shoulders bowed; these are
the blocks of ice which have never melted.

You have painted a suspension bridge across the void,
A swift boat lies in wait: Did you plan to
bring the unfortunate here?

Sonnet Fifteen

Look! Caravans of loaded horses
Merchandise from far away places;
Water washes dirt and sand
from those nameless places far away.

The wind, a thousand miles away, will
sweep with sighs of foreign lands:
We have passed many mountains and rivers,
Now possessing them, now leaving them behind.

Like a bird, fluttering in the sky,
Ruling the airy void forever,
Forever feeling, ruling nothingness.

Reality . . .what is it?
Nothing can be brought from faraway places,
Nothing can be taken away from here.

Sonnet Sixteen

Side by side on a lofty peak
we stand, becoming
the vast plain before us
With its criss-crossing paths.

Which river or road is not connected?
Which wind or cloud does not call to the other?
Cities, mountains, rivers we have passed
become our very lives.

Our growth, our griefs,
A pine tree on some distant slope,
Or thick mist over a city,

We follow the blast of the wind, the flow of water,
Becoming criss-crossing paths on the plain,
Becoming the lives of travellers on these paths.

Sonnet Seventeen

You say you like watching
These life-filled paths on the plain,
Paths vivified by footsteps,
Trodden by men without names.

Tangled pathways
In the heart's wilderness,
Impressed by those who have gone nowhere:

Lonely children, white-haired couples,
Youth
And friends now dead.

All have walked out their paths;
Retread these steps
that the paths will not be left to the wilderness.

Sonnet Eighteen

We often spend an intimate night
In an unfamiliar room, what it looks like
In daytime, we cannot tell, less can we
say about its past and future. Wilderness

Boundlessly spreads outside our window,
We can scarcely remember the road we came at dusk.
That is all we know,
Tomorrow we'll leave, and will not return.

Close your eyes! In our hearts
Let these intimate nights be woven
into unfamiliar places. Outside the window

Our lives are like the wilderness in which
our eyes blurred with a tree, or a flash of the lake.
Its vastness hides the forgotten past, the implicit future.

Sonnet Nineteen

A wave, we part from one another,
Our world divided into two.
Feeling cold, our eyes now widen.
two newborn infants.

Separation, birth.
We bear the toils of work,
Changing the cold to warmth,
Making acquaintances out of strangers;
Each one must till his field,

In order to meet again; as on the first occasion,
We're grateful for memories of the past;
As on the first occasion, we thought about our former lives.

How many springs and winters are there to a lifetime?
We can only feel the turn of the seasons,
Not the limited span of life.

Sonnet Twenty

How many faces, voices,
So real in our dreams;

They are my life's disintegrations—
Intimate, or strange.

Is it not that lives are composed
And bloom to fruitage?
Who can steer his life
Before such an endless night?

Who can let his voice and face
linger only in some cosy dreams?
How many times have we been

Seen in the broad sky—
Refreshing dreams for the boatmen,
Or desert travellers.

Sonnet Twenty-one

Listening to the storm in gusty winds,
Under the lamplight, we, lonesome.
In this small cottage,
Between our utensils

There is a vast difference:
The copper kettle belongs to the mountain ore,
The porcelain pitcher belongs to the river clay.
Like frightened birds in a tempest,

Each goes its own way.
We embrace, helplessly.
The gale sweeps things up to the sky,

The storm flushes things back to earth.
Only this flimsy lamp
Proves our temporal existence.

Sonnet Twenty-two

Deep night, deep mountain,
Listen to the heavy night rain.
Ten miles away, a mountain village,
Twenty miles away, a tumultous city.

Do they still exist?
Rivers, mountains, ten years ago,
Dreams, fancies, twenty years ago
All buried in the rain.

Strait surroundings
A return to the womb;
Deep in the night a prayer

Like a primal man:
God, give my strait heart
a vast universe.

Sonnet Twenty-three

Rain has fallen continuously for half a month;
Since you were born
You've only known the dismal, the gloomy.
One day, rain clouds suddenly disperse

and sunlight beams over the wall.
I see your mother then,
Lifting you in her jaws to the sunrays

Letting you feel the light and warmth for the first time.
And at sunset, she brings you
in again. You haven't

a memory, but the experience
will manifest itself, when some day you'll
bark and bring forth light in the dark of night.

Sonnet Twenty-four

Here, a thousand years ago
Everywhere, our lives seemed
to have been
Before we were born.

A song had already been sung
from the elusive sky,
From green grass and pines
about our fate.

We are burdened by hardships
here, how can we hear
such a song?

Look, the tiny insect
in its flight,
It is eternity all the time.

Sonnet Twenty-five

Stationery on the desk
Books displayed on the shelf.
Amidst these silent objects
we spend the day in thought.

There are no songs in words,
No dances in actions.
Vaguely, we wonder why the bird
outside the window flaps its wings.

Only as the body sleeps,
When the night is still, does its rhythms begin.
And air plays in the body,

And sea salt plays in the blood,
And in dreaming, can you hear
the sky, the sea calling to us?

Sonnet Twenty-six

We walk each day on a familiar road
To return to our homes,
But in these woods, there are
Concealed paths, deep and strange.

Walking a strange one, a little fear begins,
Worrying, the farther we go, the further we're lost.
Unawares, through the openings of the scattered trees,
Our home is suddenly in sight,

like a new island on the horizon.
So many things close to us
Demand new interpretations.

Don't feel that everything is familiar;
Till death comes, you touch yourself
Wondering; whose body is this?

Sonnet Twenty-seven

From a flow of the shapeless water,
The water-carrier fills his oval pitcher,
Thus so much water possesses a definite shape;
Look, how the vane flutters in the autumn wind

Holding an object that can't be held,
And let the mind, the light,
the darkness, and the growth of woods faraway,
run towards the infinite,

And preserve something of this vane!
We have listened to a night's wind,
And watched a day's yellow grass and red leaves;

Where shall we dispose our ideas?
Hope these poems will hold like a vane—
some things that cannot be held.

The author's notes:

(Sonnet Three)—The tree is Eucalyptus globulus.
(Sonnet Four)—The white grass is called Edelweiss in Germany.
(Sonnet Five)—Venice.

(Sonnet Seven)—During the air raids in Kunming, citizens hid themselves in the suburbs.

(Sonnet Nine)—To a friend who has fought on the front line all these years.

(Sonnet Ten)—Written on March 5, which is the date for the first commemoration of the death of Mr. Ts'ai Yüan-pei. The last quatrain was taken from the idea of Rilke who wrote to a certain lady in November 19, 1917, commenting on Rodin and Verhaeren.

(Sonnet Eleven)—Lu Hsün has an essay called "Awakening" in his book *Wild Grass*.

(Sonnet Twelve)—To Tu Fu.

(Sonnet Thirteen)—To Goethe.

(Sonnet Fourteen)—To van Gogh.

(Sonnet Twenty-two, last couplet)—Taken from the *Koran*.

(Sonnet Twenty-four)—A few newborn puppies.

The Dominance of
Lyrical Romanticism

In the course of the last one hundred years, romantic theory and its variations, such as those examined by M. H. Abrams,[1] have gradually found their way into China. The utilization of these theories by an emerging indigenous literary movement has resulted in striking poetic manifestations which are really neither Western nor Chinese, but instead an amalgam of elements deriving from both traditions. Moreover, modern Chinese poetry reflects both Chinese poets' understanding and their misunderstanding of romantic perspectives and aesthetic theories.

An examination of the works of these poets, and in particular, the lyric poetry of modern Chinese poets of the last fifty years, reveals characteristics which are, undoubtedly, echoes of the rallying calls of European romanticism. In Kuo Mo-jo's correspondence, for instance, we read of Kuo's emphasis on the role of the emotions rather than rationality in the creation of poetry. Poetry, he believes, is a blending of the emotions, the intuition and the imagination couched in suitable language and form. But it is the "spontaneous overflow of powerful emotions" (which Kuo metaphorically envisions as a wave stirring the images on the mind's surface) which creates " . . . its own periodicity or oscillation," driving the poet on into the act of creation with little apparent help from the rational aspects of the intellect. Kuo further asserts that it is the poet's emotions which lead to the creation of great poetry, and he somewhat sweepingly enumerates works from both the Eastern and European traditions as examples of pure, emotional outpourings.[2] While such an assertion stands, admittedly, on shaky grounds, it nevertheless reflects a recognition by modern Chinese poets of the importance of the human individual, and in particular, the importance of the poetic self. Although China has not been without a lyric tradition of its own, the European romantic movement, with its stress on the experience of the individual, presented the Chinese with a mode of thought which unequivocally sanctioned the centrality of the poet in the creation of verse. Traditionally, Chinese lyricism does indeed present an "experiencing voice," but the poetic "I" is, more often than not, a faceless entity existing outside the poetic totality.

90

Romanticism, George Poulet has pointed out, is essentially " . . . a taking possession by consciousness of the basically subjective character of the mind," adding that "the romantic is one who discovers himself to be a center."[3] That the discovery of the self as a center on the part of Chinese poets was inspired by the influx of European romanticism cannot readily be proved. Nevertheless, the tenets of European romanticism provided an impetus for Chinese poets to depart from centuries of literary as well as philosophical traditions.

Perhaps the most vital realization the romantic may count upon is the knowledge deep within himself of "something which cannot be assimilated to an object."[4] Such a knowledge, Poulet contends, leads to the recognition of " . . . the most authentic part of himself, the part which he (the poet) most willingly recognizes as his own,"[5] namely, his own subjectivity. Inevitably, the focus on the self necessitates the use of a language with which the poet may best express his vision, and such a language is hardly to be the language of other individuals, living in other times. In a parallel to the romantic notion of "man speaking to men" where the use of language was concerned, modern Chinese poets sought to free themselves from the highly stylized and concentrated language of classical Chinese poetry. These poets opted for the modern spoken idiom as the vehicle for their newly found subjectivity. With the abandonment of the traditionally sanctioned poetic language came a search for new poetic forms which attempted to integrate the poetics of both Europe and China and which achieved varying degrees of success.

In the light of China's literary history, it can be said that the romantic orientation was perhaps inevitable. Whether romanticism itself is necessarily European and thus, a purely external influence, is of small consequence. There are Chinese poets who acknowledge a direct debt to the European tradition and who, like Kuo Mo-jo, wished unabashedly to emulate European models. In Kuo's poem in the *Creation* journal, for instance, he says:

> I call upon the poets of the Chou,
> The literary giants of Ch'u,
> The poetry masters of T'ang,
> The playwrights of Yuan
> To become the Indian poet of the *Bhagavad Gita!*
> The Dante of the *Divine Comedy!*
> The Milton of *Paradise Lost!*
> The Goethe of *Faust!*[6]

Chinese literature, however, has always tended, as Hu Shih indicated, to discard poetic modes which failed to serve the poet's needs. From the time of the ancient *Book of Songs*, Hu noted, there has always been a shift away from the language and forms grown "unnatural" with the passage of time and change, to modes which afford greater leeway and in which the individual can better express his or her poetic sensibilities.[7]

The reasons for this receptiveness to the concept of individualism, coming when it did to China, are material for a study which lies more in the socio-philosophical arena. But as Chu Kuang-ch'ien observes, "literature is the life expression of the whole race,"[8] and any literature, as such, represents an integrated effort of the poet's creative mind as well as his distinctively social self. Thus, in spite of the focus on the poet himself in modern Chinese lyricism, his subjectivity can never be divorced from the impact his environment and the uniquely Chinese tradition has on him. Like his European counterparts, the Chinese poet, imbued now with a sense of the integrity of an inner self, becomes aware of a " . . . historical self, which is a sense of the timeless as well as of the temporal and of the timeless and of the temporal together."[9] With a subjectivity which has its links to both the poet's times and to generations of other consciousnesses, it thus stands to reason that René Wellek's suggestion that general definitions of the lyric be abandoned in favor of a turning instead " . . . to the history and thus description of genres which can be grasped in their concrete conventions and tradition" was observed.[10] The lyricism which has emerged from the European romantic movement, in other words, has no bearing on the lyricism connected with the "romantic" overviews of the modern Chinese poet. Thus, such definitions as those of Burke[11] and Hernadi,[12] while providing certain critical tools for the examination of these Chinese lyrics, tend to become inapplicable when clearly defined characteristics associated with European romanticism are blurred by purely Chinese perspectives.

In Kuo Mo-jo's excessively dithyrambic outpourings and literary ideas, we see evidence of Spinoza's romanticism coupled with a sense of Whitmanesque heroism. In keeping with European romanticism, Kuo's view of the world tends towards a pantheism shaped primarily by the poet's own subjectivity. However, the most important aspect of romanticism felt by this generation of Chinese poets lay, perhaps, not so much in the direct borrowings and imitations of European and American poets as in their discovery of highly metaphoric verse. In tracing the development of modern Chinese verse, Chu Tzu-ch'ing places symbolic poetry at the end of a progression which begins with free verse, runs through regulated verse and peaks with symbolic poetry. In an article called "The Progression of Poetry," Chu adds that literature of the classical tradition does not lend itself easily to the search for secondary levels of meaning and the lack of a poetic tradition written in a spoken idiom has, hitherto, prevented the development of symbolic verse. Chinese free verse, Chu contends, unhampered by the strictures of poetics, has resulted in a looseness of expression which inevitably renders the works pedestrian. On the other hand, Chu notes that modern regulated verse tends to be "Platonic instead of realistic" regarding the theme of love.[13]

In Pien Chih-lin's poem "The Flute," which has been criticized for its "lack of social value" and "mundane melancholy,"[14] the extended use of metaphor successfully captures the nuances of loneliness while giving the work a poetic cohesiveness. New meanings, as Philip Wheelright would have it, emerge as metaphors suggesting various levels of experience are juxtaposed.[15]

> Like a migratory bird holding a foreign seed
>   in its beak,
> The tri-masted boat brings a flute.
> Through sunset, through the western sea,
> The Ch'ang-an Maru brings a man
>   from west of the sea.
> Hearing the flute of a drunk man downstairs at midnight,
> He thinks of a foreigner's sojourn in a lonely retreat.
> Having heard the cries of the wild geese,
>   sadness is aroused,
> He obtains consolation from his neighbor's flute.
> Next morning, in the festivity of the Ch'ang-an city,
> He alone seeks for a mournful bamboo . . .
> (Why among flowers of the New Year lanterns
> There flows a strand of sad classic fragrance?)
> Return, return, return!
> Like a migratory bird holding a foreign seed
>   in its beak,
> The tri-masted boat brings a flute.
> And the flute has become a plant in Japan.
> (Why among flowers of the New Year lanterns,
> There flows a strand of sad classic fragrance?)
> Return, return, return!
> Do you wish to bring back the lost grievances, you,
>   man of the western sea?[16]

In this poem, a tri-masted boat comes into port "like a migratory bird," and by placing the image of the migratory bird alongside the boat in the harbor, Pien immediately establishes a sense of evanescence which is the key to the poem's theme of human isolation. Like a bird migrating with the seasons, the "man of the western sea" who is aboard the boat must experience the loneliness which comes from not having any established roots. He floats and flows like a bamboo or a flute drifting from one place to another. Alone, away from home at midnight, the wanderer hears the forlorn music of another flutist who has attempted to alleviate his feelings with wine. Sharing the feeling of loneliness in the New Year's Eve, the wanderer imperceptibly echoes to a deeper tragic sense of isolation. Consequently, the next morning, New Year's day (a day for family reunions), he searches for the flutist amidst the festivities of the ancient city. However, the stranger soon realizes that new mornings or new years, bring no relief for human loneliness: "among flowers of New Year lanterns/ There flows a strand of sad classic fragrance." His subsequent search for another lonely stranger on the first day of the new year allows him to see in his fruitless effort that loneliness transcends the boundaries of both time and space. The reference to "the festivity of the Ch'ang-an city" is particularly crucial in connection with this notion, for Ch'ang-an is both the ancient city which was destroyed, as well as Kyoto, which was modelled after the old Chinese capital. In every age and geographical location, humans are thus in a sense sojourners, wandering over the face of the earth like migratory birds and wild geese.

It is this central theme which most identifies Pien with the romanticism of the West, for the romantic is the poet whose "pleasure . . .in inserting himself in the universe is no longer that of feeling himself at home, but rather of feeling himself displaced."[17] The central metaphor of humanity's transient existence is effectively projected by the shift in focus from one metaphoric vehicle to another, from the migratory bird to the tri-masted boat, from the flute aboard the Ch'ang-an Maru to the festivity in the Ch'ang-an city. In Pien's work, we thus see keynotes of lyricism associated traditionally with the lyric poetry of the Western tradition, for the poem indeed "moves from image to image," while following " . . . its own inimitable progression, acting through variations and expansions of themes, changes in rhythm and elaborations of images to reach a point of greatest intensity at which the poet's vision is realized."[18]

In a poem entitled "Prophecy" by Ho Ch'i-fang, written in 1931, the subjective intensity of the poet's imagination provides the focal point as well as the dynamic force of the work.

> This heart-throbbing day finally arrives.
> The sound of your footsteps approaches,
>   like night sighs.
> I can hear distinctly that they are
>   not forest leaves' whispers,
>   nor night winds,
> Nor subtle steps of deer darting along mossy paths.
> Tell me, tell me with your ringing voice,
> Aren't you the young deity in the prophecy?
>
> You must have come from the warm and exuberant south,
> Tell me about the moonlight, the sun's rays,

Tell me how spring winds open a hundred flowers,
How sparrows are infatuated with green willows,
I shall close my eyes and sleep
  in your dreamy songs,
Such warmth and comfort, I seem to remember,
  and yet, seem to forget.

Please pause, pause in your tiring journey,
Please enter, here is a tiger hide for you to rest,
Let me burn the leaves I gathered in autumn,
And hear me softly sing my song.
My singing will dip and rise like burning flames,
Like burning flames, it will tell
  the life of the fallen leaves.

Advance not, the jungle ahead is boundless,
Aged trees bearing motley designs of beasts,
Like serpents, languid vines interwine,
Dense foliage refuses a star to seep through.
When you hear the empty echo of your first step,
Timidly, you won't dare to move your second step.

Must you leave? Let me accompany you then;
My feet know every safe path.
I will incessantly sing you unwearied songs,
And offer my hands of warmth and comfort.
When pitch darkness falls upon us,
You may fix your eyes on mine.

You pay no attention to my emotional singing,
Nor will your feet pause for my trembling.
Like a serene breeze passing through the evening,
Your proud footsteps vanish . . .
Oh, have you really come silently, like
  the prophecy once told,
And silently left, my young deity?[19]

In this poem we find that vernacular Chinese can be used in ways which
work toward the various stages of the lyric progression. As each image is
touched upon, Ho boldly intensifies and expands each new level of meaning
through the use of repetition. The repeated use of the phrase "Tell me," in
the first two stanzas, for instance, produces an insistent impact which drives
the poem forward from one connecting image to the next with an urgency
which lets up only as the third verse opens with words "Please
pause . . . pause in your tiring journey."

In the remaining verses, the use of repeated words and phrases like the
lines "My song will dip and rise like burning flames,/ Like burning flames it
will tell of the life of the fallen leaves" continues to effect the movement

which will bring the poem to its close. But the sense of urgency here has diminished and effectively parallels the poet's own sense of diminished expectations. All of the mind's avid desire to pursue the mystery of moonlight, the sun's rays and the blossoming of a hundred flowers remains finally unrealized. The elusive moment of revelation when all things are intensely clarified slips away beyond the mind's conscious reach. That many of Ho's novel turns of phrases are awkward is undoubtedly true in terms of Chinese traditional syntax. By employing in the Chinese vernacular repetitions and reversed syntactical arrangements of words characteristic of European poetry, Ho has managed to give his poem the elasticity so necessary to the sense of consecution of lyricism.

With the Japanese invasion of China in the 1930s, a different artistic direction was to govern the modern poetic movement. The symbolism of Li Chin-fa, Wang Tu-ch'ing and Yu Keng-yu gave way to a mode which combined characteristics of both the heroic and the lyric. Emerging from a tradition which began at the turn of the century, the poetry of Wen I-to, Tai Wang-shu, Ai Ch'ing and T'ien Chien reflected a far more robust optimism in the face of difficult times than did the works of their precursors. In contrast to the self-indulgent overtones of the "Crescent Moon" and the modernist school, with their penchant for the lurid and the sensational , the poets of the Sino-Japanese War era exhibit a wholesomeness in their patriotism which is often evident in their compositions. Tai Wang-shu's "I Use My Maimed Hands," for instance, is an ardent outcry against the Japanese enslavement of China, while Wen I-to's "A Phrase" provides a rallying call for a unified nation.

Thus when Li Ou-fan speaks of China as being deluged by an entire tradition of European romanticism in the short span of a decade (1920–30),[20] he may be speaking of the transitional stage in which Chinese poets progressed from the intensely personal lyricism characteristic of both English and American romanticism towards a "gothic"[21] lyricism characterized by noble and humanistic aspirations, which ultimately reflect the futility of all human endeavor, and which are more Western than Chinese in tone and sentiment. Despite these tendencies, we may say that the emergence of this rather controversial kind of lyric poetry, particularly the modernist verse of poets like Ho Ch'i-fang, Pien Chih-lin and Feng Chih, has undoubtedly contributed to the formation of a new genre of poetry in modern Chinese literature.

The Polemics of New Forms

Early in the development of modern Chinese poetry the choice of an appropriate form provided a serious point of debate among the major poets. Essentially, the movement sought to free itself from the stringent rules of poetry writing associated with the classical modes. The major contention of the modern poets was that the imposition of rigid forms tended to hamper the free flow of expression. On the other hand, it was recognized that casting off time honored rules did not necessarily imply a gravitation toward total formlessness. It was clearly a matter of, figuratively speaking, finding new bottles for new wine rather than to attempt to employ old vessels.

One of the earliest, and perhaps the most vocal, advocates of the need for form in modern poetry was Wen I-to. In keeping with traditional thought, Wen believed that a good poet, if he were ingenious enough, could accommodate his material artistically within the limitations presented by the structural conventions of poetry. There is, he said, in poetic creation, the lure of having to pit one's ability against a set of established rules and eventually emerging victorious. According to Wen, the proficient poet is one who is willing to "dance in shackles." He further asserted that "only those who don't know how to write poetry will feel the bondage of form."[1] In other words, a poem consists of the poet's free play of expression within the circumscribed limitations of form. The prescribed forms of antiquity, Wen felt, were suitable vehicles to express a past existence. Even when the modern poets were seeking newer modes of expression in the light of changing subjectivities, they could not totally divorce themselves from older forms. In advocating the symmetrical alignment of characters, thereby producing a visually symmetrical poem, Wen essentially adhered to both the classical precepts of poetic composition and to the forms of Western and particularly English poetry.

However, Fu Tung-hua argued that the "pictorial" nature of the Chinese written characters and the alignment of characters into architecturally pleasing forms can hinder an organic approach to poetry:

> We should know that the vitality of the poetic language . . . does not lie in the form of the words, but in the image that the form represents . . . . This is why we must not

97

be hindered by the form of the language when we read poetry. Instead, we should use the eye of the mind to approach directly the image hidden in its form.[2]

The central meaning of any poem, cannot be divorced from the construction of the poem which has been built around it. The substantial structure, in turn, cannot exist simply for itself but must both point to and reflect the central vision. The physical eye perceives the enclosing structure of the poem, but it is the "mind's eye" taking its cue from what the physical eye perceives, which directs attention to the core of the poem. Only as meaning is apprehended can there be a movement away from the structural limitation of the poem.

According to Wen's dictum, rhythms must be determined by the symmetrical arrangement of words. Ho Ch'i-fang, a staunch advocate of "modern formulative verse," suggests not a symmetrical arrangement of words but rather a symmetrical alignment of spaces between word groups.[3] Rhythm is determined thus by the regular pauses taken during the progression of each line. Ho's contention is that the metrical patterns of the classical lyric meters or verse were formulated according to the regular pauses between word groups rather than according to the arrangement of the words *per se*, words being made up of either two or three Chinese characters, each representing one syllable. However, Ho points out that the patterns of pauses used by the classical poets are much too rigid to be adopted in modern formulative verse. Adherents of this school saw the necessity of functioning within the rules, like that of symmetrically aligning the pauses between word groups. By the same token, Ho and his followers recognized too that these pauses could not come from merely fitting words together to make up an architecturally pleasing structure, but that the natural rhythms and music of the spoken tongue must be incorporated into modern Chinese poetry. By structuring a poem on an essentially mathematical basis, Wen I-to, according to Ho, neglected the interaction between poetic expression and the nature of the Chinese language, thereby restricting severely the free flow of expression.

In pursuing a poetic expression based on the rhythms of contemporary spoken Chinese, Ho Ch'i-fang turns to the Chinese popular ballad form as an example of verse form established on the regulation of pauses. In terms of Wen's mathematical symmetry of words, these ballads are, by comparison, irregular and structurally asymmetrical. The pauses are not determined by the number of characters grouped into word units, but by natural units of meaning. The location of breaks is determined, presumably, by customary usage and the generally accepted function of the word within its poetic context. It is here that Ho's theory runs into difficulty, since several obstacles stand in the way of arbitrarily fixing the order of the pauses in order to construct a rhythmically satisfying poem. Foremost amongst these is the change which has taken place in the Chinese language itself since classical times. The obvious additions in Chinese are the pronouns. Devoid of prepositions, verbs and conjunctions, the pauses made between units of meaning are simple enough in the classical version: however, the introduction of pronouns in the modern rendition raises the possibility of several rhythmic patterns depending on where one chooses to place the stresses and the pauses. Determining where to place a stress or a pause becomes highly subjective, though ironically enough, the additional parts of speech which have come to be used in the modern Chinese idiom have not rendered specificity or clarity to meaning but have, instead, opened the way to variations of possible meanings. Since poetic stress is so closely linked to meaning and meaning has, by virtue of changes in the language, become more open to subjectivity, it becomes virtually impossible to posit definitive formulae for the construction of metrical patterns. Even Ho's adherence to the ballad formula as to where stresses and pauses are to be placed cannot, in all instances, provide the modern poet with a reliable standard to follow.

In addition, the structural definition of the ballad can determine the rhythmic pattern of a work, but it does so only in terms of a quasi-musical rendition of the poem. The Chinese ballad form is associated primarily with an oral tradition. Metrical patterns formulated according to the stresses and pauses of the ballad, while natural enough when chanted or sung, often seem unnatural when rendered as poetry to be read. The stilted nature of ballad rhythm in modern Chinese poetry becomes particularly apparent when stress is placed on the experimental and internal vision in which poetry is mostly read in silence.

Thus, the ballad form offers little to the modern poet by way of metrical formulae, but it does represent a break with the rigid restrictions of classical poetry, in its departure from both the standard subjects and forms employed by the classical poets. Like modern Chinese poetry, the ballad stresses the use of the spoken idiom and has, as its focus, the expression of various aspects of human experience. Characteristically, it is the ballad's movement away from the classical requirements of structure and content that modern Chinese poets and critics alike most admire. The critic-linguist Wang Li, for instance, draws a parallel between the departure of modern Chinese poetry from older forms and the ballad's independence of classical poetry. He sees that the forces leading toward greater self-expression in both movements are akin to the forces which led to the creation of free verse.[4]

In searching for guidelines upon which metrical patterns could be drawn, the early modern Chinese poets did not hesitate to attempt to apply metrical patterns borrowed from Western, and particularly, English verse. Among those who turned to the West in hopes of discovering definitive rules for the establishment of regular verse patterns was Lu Chih-wei, who experimented with iambic pentameter as a formulaic basis for rhythms in modern Chinese verse.

According to Lu, stress is placed on substantive words, while less emphasis is borne by functional words. Lu further designates the unit between two stressed syllables (substantive words), as a metrical foot, and with five intervals between the stressed syllables, he managed to compose Chinese verse in the iambic, and on occasion, the trochaic pentameter.[5]

The most serious flaw in Lu's theory is perhaps his disregard for the obvious differences between the English and Chinese languages. The iambic, or "walking rhythm," is inherent in the English language, and except for the rather vague and sweeping observation that "the tone of the Chinese language is very similar to the tone of the English language,"[6] he gives little consideration to the problems of accommodating the Chinese language, with its own linguistic distinctions, to an English verse form. To all intents and purposes, his theory of poetic rhythm is based on an instinctive knowledge of where stressed and unstressed syllables are to be placed in a poem, notwithstanding his theory of functional and substantive words.

A difficulty arises in knowing which syllable of a bi- or tri-syllabic word specifically to stress while reading a line of Chinese poetry. Unlike multi-syllabic English words where the stressed and unstressed syllables are rather well defined, multi-syllabic Chinese words can bear their stressed and unstressed syllables on practically any syllable depending on the context in which the word is placed. In Lu's own poem "Pentametric Variations,"[7] the line "Evening is the time for dreams to go out of doors" contains three two-character words, or three words each having two syllables, namely, *huang-hun* (evening), *ch'u-men* (go out of doors) and *shih-hou* (time). All of the words are substantive words and if Lu's rule of stress is to be followed, both syllables in each word should be stressed. In placing the stress on, say, the first word "evening" (*huang-hun*), however, does one stress "*huang*" or "*hun*" or both, since no ground rule exists. (Compare to the English equivalent "eve-ning" where the stress is always on "eve" rather than on the "-ning.") The same problem also occurs with the other two words in this line from Lu's poem.

What can be seen in Lu Chih-wei's verse is that his stress patterns are linked to the intensity of his poetic expression rather than to any of the theories he has tried to establish. Stressed and unstressed syllables are used very much in conjunction with his poetic instincts. Given the fluidity of Chinese words regarding the placement of stress, an exercise such as that which Lu has attempted is possible. His verses are approximations of pentametric verse. His difficulties arise, however, primarily from his attempt to formulate a comprehensive formula of poetic rhythms based on the flimsiest of notions of linguistic distinctions. In his own poetry, it is his use of rhymes—direct rhymes, slant rhymes and internal rhymes—which provides the basis of poetic cohesion.

The directions modern Chinese poets took in patterning their verse after Western modes were not restricted to their imitation of metrical pattern alone. In Wang Li's *Versification of the Chinese Language*,[8] two distinct poetic forms of modern Chinese poetry are recognized, the *"pai-hua,"* a Chinese equivalent of Western free verse, and the so-called "Europeanized" poetry or verse modelled after traditional Western verse.

The definition Wang Li gives for free verse amounts to little beyond the fact that it is poetry which is free from the regulations governing conventional verse. In the absence of rhymed stanzas, Wang Li notes the repetition of words and phrases which characterizes the free verse of both contemporary Western poets as well as similar attempts on the part of modern Chinese poets. The use of repetitive sounds, Wang believes, compensates for the absence of rhyme as a means of achieving poetic cohesion. But beyond these observations, Wang fails to examine the functions of the words and phrases which are repeated in both Western and Chinese free verse. In reviewing some examples of modern Chinese free verse, we find that the repetition of certain words does not function simply, as Wang Li asserts, as a compensation for the absence of rhyme and meter. The repetition of key words can also serve to disclose secondary meanings, just as it can amplify and extend the central vision of the poem. The sense of resolution provided by the matching of similar sounds in rhymed verse is matched in free verse by either the repetition of a word or by its use as a different part of speech.

Thus we see the diverging polemics on new forms are, in fact, conceptualized practices of European influences on the one hand, and struggles to adhere to Chinese tradition on the other. Wen I-to's architectural theory of symmetrical structure echoes in its concreteness with Fu T'ung-hua's imagistic consciousness of the Chinese language. Despite the failures of Ho Ch'i-fang and Lu Chih-wei in their advocacy of formulative pauses and stresses, they nevertheless reflected a theoretical struggle for new Europeanized forms in order to accomodate their new Europeanized practices. Hence, the struggles for a new form among these poets and critics should be viewed as a quest in which the poet extended himself not so much in the sense of new discovery, but rather in finding a harmonious coexistence between the idea he wished to express and the way it was expressed.

Notes and References

Chapter One

1. See *Chung-kuo hsin wen-hsueh ta-hsi (Modern Chinese Literature Compendium)*, ed. Chao Chia-pi (Shanghai, 1936), pp. 75–76, 78–80. Hereafter cited as *Ta-hsi*.

2. Mao Tun, "Kuan-yu 'Wen-hsueh yen-chiu hui' " ("About the 'Literary Research Association' "), *Ta-hsi*, X, p. 89.

3. *Ibid.*, p. 89.

4. Ch'eng Fang-wu, "Hsieh-shih chu-i yu yung-su chu-i" ("Realism and Trivialism"), *Ta-hsi*, II, p. 195.

5. *Ibid.*, p. 196.

6. Wang Yao, *Chung-kuo hsin-wen-hsueh shih kao (Draft History of China's New Literature)* (Peking, 1949, rpt., Hong Kong, 1972), p. 44. Hereafter cited as *Shih Kao*.

7. *Ta-hsi*, IV "Introduction," p. 5.

8. *Ibid.*, pp. 5–6.

9. *Ibid.*, p. 6.

10. Ch'en Hsiang-ho, "Kuan-yu 'Ch'en-chun she' ti kuo-ch'u hsien-tsai chi chiang-lai" ("About the Past, Present and Future of the 'Sunken Bell Society' "), *Ta-hsi*, X, p. 198.

11. *Ibid.*, p. 199.

12. *Ibid.*, p. 199.

13. See Wang Yao, p. 75.

14. Mao Tse-tung, "Chung-kuo kung-ch'an-tang tsai min-chu chan-cheng ti ti-wei" ("The Position of the Chinese Communists in the National War"), in *Chung-kuo hsien-tai wen hsueh shih ts'an-k'ao tzu-liao (Research Materials on the History of Modern Chinese Literature)*, ed. Peking Shih-fan ta-hsueh Chung-wen-hsi hsien-tai wen-hsueh chiao-hsueh kai-ke hsiao-tsu (Committee on Revision of the Teaching of Modern Literature, Department of Chinese Literature, Peking Normal University) (Peking, 1960), I, no. 2., p. 725. Hereafter cited as *Ts'an-kao tzu-liao*.

15. Hsiang Lin-ping's articles were later collected in *Min-chu hsing-shih t'ao-lun chi (Discussions on National Form)*, ed. Hu Feng (Chungking). Since the book is out of print, I have obtained the information from Wang,

shih kao; and Li Huo-jen, "Ho Ch'i-fang p'ing-ch'uan" ("On Ho Ch'i-fang"),*Po-wen Monthly,* I, no. 5.(1974), p. 58.

16. This view is presented in Mao Tun's speech delivered at the All-China Conference of Writers, July, 1949. See *shih kao,* p. 28.

17. Mao Tse-tung, "Tsai Yen-an wen-i tso-t'an hui-shang ti chiang-hua" ("Talks at the Yenan Forum on Literature and Art"), *Ts'an-k'ao tzu-liao,* I No. 2., pp. 24–25. See also D. T. Fokkema, *Literary Doctrine in China and Soviet Influence 1956–1960* (Hague, 1965), pp. 3-10; and Merle Goldman, *Literary Dissent in Communist China* (Cambridge, 1967), pp. 1–17.

18. *Ibid.*; see also *Ts'an-k'ao tzu-liao.* The translations of Mao's talks I quote in this chapter are from Fokkema's partial translation that appear in his discussion of Mao's talks. See Fokkema, p. 5.

19. Feng Chih, *Shih-nien shih ch'ao (Poetry In Ten Years)* (Peking, 1959), p. 104. Feng insisted that "The birth of New China has made every Chinese to experience a new birth. I again used my spare time to write and made poetry an inseparable part of my life. The tone of these poems is basically different from that of the past. Now, it is confident, optimistic, and it extols the Chinese Communist Party, and the great achievements under the Party's leadership. It also satirizes and attacks the enemy of the people."

20. Feng Chih, "Hsin shih ti hsing-shih wen-t'i" ("Problems of Form in New Poetry") in *Shih yu i-ch'an (Poetry And Legacy)* (Peking, 1963), p. 143.

21. *Ibid.,* p. 143.

Chapter Two

1. Feng Chih's splendid poems not only caused Lu Hsun to call him "the most distinguished lyricist" (see "Introduction," *Ta-hsi,* IV, p. 5), but Lu Hsun also included two short stories by Feng in *Ta-hsi* indicating an appreciation of Feng's talents as a writer of prose fiction.

2. Chu Kuang-ch'ien, "Hsien-tai Chung-kuo wen-hsueh" ("Modern Chinese Literature"), *Wen-hsueh tsa-chih (Literature),* 2, No. 8 (1948), p. 15.

3. *Ibid.,* p. 15.

4. *Ibid.,* p. 16.

5. *Ta-hsi,*VIII, pp. 340–41.

6. Feng Chih, "I Can Only Sing," in *Feng Chih shih-wen hsuan-chi (Selected Prose and Poems of Feng Chih)* (Peking, 1955), pp. 14–15.

7. "Northern Expedition," *ibid.,* p. 70.

8. *Ibid.,* p. 1.

9. Pien Chih-lin, "Broken Chapter," in *Yu-mu Chi (Collection of False Pearls)* (Shanghai, 1935), p. 12.

10. Ho Ch'i-fang, *Shih-ko hsin-shang (Appreciation of Poetry)* (Peking, 1962), p. 92. Ho concludes that "although such affection towards vigorous

objects and such touching praises were initiated by the passion of love, their meanings have already surpassed the realm of love."

11. Ao Ao, "Shih-jen yu k'uei-lei" ("The Poet and the Puppet") *Ch'i-ling nien-tai yueh-pao (Seventies Monthly)* (May, 1971), pp. 22–24.

12. Kai-yu Hsu, "Introduction," *Twentieth Century Chinese Poetry: An Anthology* (Ithaca, 1963), pp. xxv, xxvi.

13. *Ibid.*, p. xxvi.

14. Feng Chih, "Southern Night," *Hsien-tai shih-hsuan (Anthology of Modern Poetry)*, ed. Shih-chieh shu-chu (Singapore, 1963), p. 44.

15. Pien Chih-lin, "White Conch," *Hsien-tai Chung-kuo shih-hsuan 1919–1949 (Modern Chinese Poetry, An Anthology 1919–1949)*, ed. M. M. Y. Fung *et al.*, I (Hong Kong, 1974), pp. 754–56. Hereafter cited as *Hsien-tai Chung-kuo shih-hsuan*.

16. Feng Chih, "Snake," in *Feng Chih Shih-wen hsuan-chi*, pp. 80–81.

17. "Fig," *ibid.*, p. 11.

18. "Evening Paper," *ibid.*, p. 10.

19. See *Hsien-tai shih-hsuan*, p. 43. Since this anthology was edited by the Shih-chieh shu-chu (World Bookstore) management in Singapore, the name of the commentator is not available.

20. Ho Ch'i-fang, "Remnant of 'Northern China Is Burning,' " *Hsien-tai Chung-kuo shih-hsuan*, pp. 677–78. Part of Ho's poem reads as follows:

> Evening paper! Evening paper!
> Every paper reports the fall of Wuhan.
> The news makes me tremble:
> People old and young
> Pushing one another on the sidewalks,
> Running:
> In darkness, red firelights blazing,
> Wooden houses exploding and crackling,
> Explosion of concrete houses,
> Distinctly heard. . .

21. Northrop Frye, *Anatomy of Criticism: Four Essays* (Princeton, 1957), p. 304. Frye also contends that "the romancer deals with individuality, with characters in *vacuo* idealized by revery, and, however conservative he may be, something nihilistic and untameable is likely to keep breaking out of his pages." *Ibid.*, p. 305.

22. "The romance tends to be introverted and personal: it also deals with characters, but in a more subjective way." *Ibid.*, p. 308.

23. Leon Edel comments on the "romantic hero" as one who "began by contemplating his heart; he ended by contemplating his mind. And he discovered that heart, symbol of feeling and perception, and mind, symbol

of thought and reason, could be closely related." See Leon Edel, *The Psychological Novel* (New York, 1964), p. 27.

24. Feng Chih, "Man-t'an hsin-shih nu-li ti fang-hsiang" ("A Casual Talk on the Aim of the New Poetry"), *Wen-i pao (Literary Journal)*, 9 (1958), p. 6.

25. See S. H. Ch'en, "Metaphor and the Conscious in Chinese Poetry under Communism," *The China Quarterly*, 13 (1963), p. 49, rpt. in *Chinese Communist Literature*, ed. Cyril Birch (New York, 1963), p. 156.

26. Feng Chih, "Our West Suburb," in *Shih-nien shih ch'ao*, p. 25.

27. "My Thanks," *ibid.*, p. 10.

28. Feng Chih, "Po Ai Ch'ing ti 'liao-chieh tso-chia, tsun-chung tso-chia'" ("A Rebuttal on Ai Ch'ing's 'Understanding Writer, Respecting Writer'"); *Wen-i pao*, 2 (1958), p. 23.

29. *Ibid.*, p. 23.

Chapter Three

1. Feng Chih, "Preface," in *Shih-ssu-hang chi (Collected Sonnets)*, 2nd edition (Shanghai, 1949), p. ii.

2. The following table shows the rhyming schemes in the twenty-seven sonnets:

Sonnet One	abba	cdcd	efg	efg
Sonnet Two	abba	acca	ded	ede
Sonnet Three	abba	cddc	eff	cgg
Sonnet Four	abba	acca	dee	daa
Sonnet Five	abba	cddc	efe	fgg
Sonnet Six	abba	cddc	efe	fgg
Sonnet Seven	abab	cdcd	cce	eff
Sonnet Eight	abab	cdcd	efg	efg
Sonnet Nine	abab	cdcd	bbe	ebe
Sonnet Ten	abba	cddc	efc	aec
Sonnet Eleven	abba	cddc	dcd	cee
Sonnet Twelve	abab	abba	ccd	cde
Sonnet Thirteen	abba	cddc	efg	efg
Sonnet Fourteen	abab	cdcd	eef	ggf
Sonnet Fifteen	abab	cdcd	eef	ggf
Sonnet Sixteen	abab	abab	cdd	cbb
Sonnet Seventeen	abab	abab	bab	bab
Sonnet Eighteen	abba	cbbc	aba	cbc
Sonnet Nineteen	abba	cddc	efg	efg
Sonnet Twenty	abab	cdcd	eff	egg
Sonnet Twenty-one	abab	acac	dde	ded
Sonnet Twenty-two	abba	cddc	eef	ggf
Sonnet Twenty-Three	abab	cdcd	eff	gff
Sonnet Twenty-Four	abba	bccb	cde	cde

Sonnet Twenty-Five	abba	cddc	eee	eff
Sonnet Twenty-Six	abba	baab	cac	dad
Sonnet Twenty-Seven	abba	acca	dde	daa

3. Walter A. Strauss, *Descent and Return* (Cambridge, 1971), pp. 9–10.

4. *Ibid.*, pp. 9–10.

5. See *Shih-ssu-hang chi*, p. ii. Feng writes that in the autumn after he finished the twenty-seven sonnets, he became ill. Although the cause of his illness is not mentioned, Feng hints that it might have resulted from his intimate contact with natural mysteries—objects in nature not supposed to be approached and contacted by humans. The "ultimate truth of nature" is not to be comprehended and revealed. Illness is often the punishment for such an offense.

6. See Rilke's letter to Xaver von Moos, April 20, 1923. Cf. Elizabeth Sewell, *The Orphic Voice* (New York, 1960), p. 373.

7. Feng Chih, "A Couplet," in *Shan-shui* (Landscape) (Shanghai, 1947), p. 21.

8. Rainer Maria Rilke, "Appendix 3," *Duino Elegies*, trans. J. B. Leishman and Stephen Spender (New York, 1967), p. 124.

9. *Shan-shui*, p. 22.

10. See Kenneth Yasuda, *The Japanese Haiku* (Tokyo, 1957), p. 183.

11. *Shan-shui*, p. 22.

12. "Sonnet One," *Shih-ssu-hang chi*, p. 3.

13. "Sonnet Five," *Sonnets to Orpheus, trans.* C. F. MacIntyre (Berkeley and Los Angeles, 1960), p. 11.

14. Strauss, p. 10.

15. *Duino Elegies*, p. 41.

16. Rainer Maria Rilke, *Letter to a Young Poet*, trans. M. D. Herter Norton (New York, 1962), p. 45.

17. See "Preface" to *Kei i-ko ch'ing-nien shih-jen te shih-feng-hsin (Ten Letters to a Young Poet)*, translation from Rainer Maria Rilke's *Briefe an einen jungen Dichter* by Feng Chih (Hong Kong, 1959), pp. 2–3.

18. Strauss, p. 178.

19. Sewell, pp. 376–77.

20. "Preface," *Shih-ssu-hang chi*, p. i.

21. "Sonnet Sixteen, " *ibid.*, p. 34.

22. William Carlos Williams, *Paterson* (New York, 1963), p. 6. Williams' popular lines read:

> — Say it, no ideas but in things —
> nothing but the blank faces of the houses
> and cylindrical trees
> bent, forked by preconception and accident —
> split, furrowed, creased, mottled, stained —
> secret — into the body of the light!

23. *Ibid.*, p. 6.

24. "The Extinct Mountain Village," *Shan-shui*, pp. 57–58.

25. *Ibid.*, pp. 57–58.

26. Robert Frost, "The Road Not Taken," in *Selected Poems of Robert Frost* (San Francisco, 1963), pp. 71–72.

Chapter Four

1. See *Ch'uang-tsao chi-k'an (Creative Quarterly)*, 2, No. 1 (1929), p. 110.

2. *Ibid.*, p. 110.

3. *Ibid.*, p. 110.

4. *Ibid.*, p. 108.

5. See Feng Chih, "Afterword on *Hsi chiao chi*, in *Shih-nien shih-ch'ao*, p. 103. This essay also appeared earlier in *Shih-k'an (Poetry Journal)*, No. 9 (1959), pp. 111-13.

6. *Ch'uang-tsao chi-k'an*, pp. 105–106.

7. Feng Chih, *Feng Chih shih-wen hsüan chi*, pp. 8–9.

8. *Ch'uang-tsao chi-k'an*, p. 98.

9. *Ibid.*, p. 99.

10. *Ibid.*, p. 99. There is a character missing in the third line of the first stanza. I have translated the line tentatively as "For the fear of overexposing its lustre."

11. *Ibid.*, p. 100.

12. *Ibid.*, p. 107.

13. *Ibid.*, p. 104.

14. See *Ta-hsi*, VIII, p. 198.

15. *Ibid.*, p. 194.

16. *Ibid.*, p. 201.

17. See Kan Pao, *Sou-shen chi (Records of Spirits)*, XIV., Shanghai, 1922, pp. 2–3. In the original version, it was not the mother who made the promise to give away her daughter. Instead, it was the maiden who ridiculed the stallion and asked it to search for her father. After her father was brought back by the stallion, she again teased the horse for its stupidity in hoping for a human spouse.

Chapter Five

1. Ai Ch'ing, "Liao-chieh tso-chia, tsun-chung tso chia" ("Understand and Respect Writers"), *Chieh-fang jih-pao* (March 11, 1942), p. 4.

2. See *Shih-nien shih-ch'ao*, p. 105.

3. *Ibid.*, p. 105.

4. *Ibid.*, p. 105.

5. *Ibid.*, p. 105.

6. See *Ts'an-k'ao tzu-liao*, III, p. 693.

7. *Ibid.*, p. 693.

8. See Chou Yang, "Hsin-min-ko k'ai-t'o liao shih-ko te hsin tao-lu" ("New Ballads Open a New Road for Poetry"), *ibid.*, p. 698.

9. See Feng Chih, "Man-t'an hsin-shih," p. 6.

10. *Ibid.*, p. 6.

11. Chou Yang, "Hsin-min-ko."

12. "To P'an Ch'ang-yu," in *Shih-nien shih-ch'ao*, pp. 22–23.

13. Chou Yang, "Hsin-min-ko."

14. "Old Hero Meng T'ai," in *Shih-nien shih-ch'ao*, pp. 31–32.

15. See Feng Chih's "Surveyors," *ibid.*, pp. 50–51. Shih-hsiang Ch'en commented on this poem by saying: " 'In front of the concentrated attention/ Nature has lost all her mysteries.' With the loss of all nature's mysteries, we would add, poetry has to lose all its depth." See Ch'en's "Metaphor and the Conscious in Chinese Poetry under Communism," *The China Quarterly*, 13 (1963), p. 46. I think the theme of exploring nature is a solidification of the poet's heroic concept. Ch'en should have been more conscious of the fact that after Liberation, the ideal hero is a commoner who can challenge and conquer nature.

16. Feng Chih, "Sonnet One", in *Shih-ssu-hang chi*, p. 3.

17. Feng Chih, "Han Po Chops Wood", in *Shih-nien shih ch'ao*, pp. 6–9. I have adopted the translation from Kai-yu Hsu's *Twentieth Century Chinese Poetry, An Anthology*, with slight modification.

18. *Ibid.*, pp. 6–9.

19. *Ibid.*, pp. 6–9.

20. Feng Chih, "A National Day Parade," in *Shih-nien shih ch'ao*, pp. 52–53.

21. Feng Chih, "Kuan-yu hsin-shih ti hsing-shih wen-t'i" ("About Problems of Form in New Poetry"), *Wen-i p'ing-lun (Criticism on Literature and Art)*, 5 (1959), p. 37.

22. *Ibid.*, p. 37.

23. "Party Living," in *Shih-nien shih ch'ao*, p. 101.

24. "Kuan-yu hsin-shih ti hsing-shih wen-t'i," p. 37.

25. Feng Chih, "Tsai wo-men ti kuo-chia li" "In Our Country," *Shih-k'an (Poetry)*, 9 (1959), p. 51.

26. Kai-yu Hsu, *The Chinese Literary Scene* (New York, 1975), p. 212. Hsu gives an interesting account of his visit with Feng Chih, his former teacher: "The questions I had saved up during the thirty years since I sat in his Rilke class all fought for expression. I wanted to know his personal experience during the literary controversies, his view on past, present, and future Chinese literature, and what his life was like at the moment. Amused by my eagerness, he urged me to have more tea and the sweets for which Peking is famous."

Appendix II

1. For a review of English romantic theory in a broad intellectual context, see M. H. Abrams, *The Mirror and the Lamp* (New York, 1953).

2. Kuo Mo-jo, "Lun shih t'ung-hsin" ("Correspondence on Poetry"), *Ta-hsi*, 1, pp. 347–349. The full text of this letter is also found in *Kuo Mo-jo shu-hsin chi (Letters of Kuo Mo-jo)* (Shanghai, 1937), pp. 1–5. I am indebted to Bonnie S. McDougall's *The Introduction of Western Literary Theories into Modern China 1919–1925* (Tokyo, 1971), particularly her detailed translation of this letter. For additional information and comments on this letter, see M. Stolzova, "The Foundations of Modern Chinese Poetics," *Archiv Orientalni*, 36 (1968), pp. 585–608.

3. George Poulet, *Les Metamorphoses du cercle* (Paris, 1961), p. 136.

4. *Ibid.*, p. 136.

5. *Ibid.*, p. 136.

6. Kuo Mo-jo, "Ch'uang-tsao che" "The Creator," *Ts'an-k'ao tzu-liao*, 1. (1928), p. 150.

7. Hu Shih, "T'an hsin-shih" ("On New Poetry"), *Ta-hsi*, 1, pp. 324–325.

8. *Wen-hsueh tsa-chih*, 2, No. 8 (1948), p. 17.

9. T. S. Eliot remarks that "a sense of the timeless as well as of the temporal and of the timeless and of the temporal together, is what makes a writer traditional. And it is at the same time what makes a writer most acutely conscious of his place in time, of his contemporaneity." See Eliot, "Tradition and Individual Talent," in *The Sacred Wood* (London, 1920), p. 49.

10. René Wellek, *Discriminations* (New Haven, 1970), p. 251. I have quoted the passage from Paul Hernadi, *Beyond Genre* (Ithaca, 1972), p. 80.

11. Kenneth Burke defines lyric as "a short complete poem, elevated or intense in thought and sentiment, expressing and evoking a unified attitude towards a momentous situation more or less explicitly implied, in diction harmonious and rhythmical, often but not necessarily rhymed, the structure leading itself readily to a musical accompaniment strongly repetitive in quality; the gratification of the whole residing in the nature of the work as an ordered summation of emotional experience otherwise fragmentary, inarticulate and unsimplified." See Burke, "Three Definitions," *The Kenyon Review*, 8 (1950), p. 174.

12. Hernadi, p. 80.

13. Chu views his classification of poetic trends rather pessimistically: "I have said in the afterthoughts of the poetry section in *Ta-hsi* that I want to see poets of an earlier stage 'liberating themselves from old shackles, learning new languages and seeking new worlds.' However, the convention is too tenacious to be broken down . . . , the singing of sensual love is, of course, different from the classical poets, however, most modern poets only touch the peripheral and stumble into cliches. . . . The love lyrics in the Modernist School are Platonic instead of realistic. At least, they are new in Chinese poetry." See Chu's *Hsin-shih tsa-hua (Diverse Talks on Poetry)* (Shanghai, 1947), pp. 10–11.

14. Ch'u I, "Hsin-shih ti tsung-chi yu ch'i ch'u-lu" ("The Tract of New Poetry and its Outlet"), *Wen-hsueh (Literature)*, 8, No. 1, p. 21.

15. Philip Wheelwright, *Metaphor and Reality* (Bloomington, 1962), p. 78.

16. Pien Chih-lin, "The Flute." The poem was published in *Ta-kung-pao shih-k'an (Poetry Section: Ta-kung Daily.)* I have quoted the poem from "Hsin-shih."

17. Helene Tuget, *Le Cosmos et l'imagination* (Paris, 1965), p. 37.

18. Ralph Freedman, *The Lyrical Novel* (Princeton, 1963), p. 7.

19. Ho Ch'i-ang, "Prophecy," in *Han-yuan Chi (Collection of the Han Garden)* (Shanghai, 1936), pp. 4–7.

20. Li Ou-fan (See also Lee, Leo Ou-fan), "Wu-ssu yun-tung yu lang-man chu-i" ("The May-Fourth Movement and Romanticism"), *Ta-hsueh tsa-chih (Intellectual Monthly)*, 53 (Taipei, 1972), p. 14.

21. Li's interpretation of romanticism as "gothic" can be traced to the Chinese articles written jointly with a fellow student at Princeton University. See Li Ou-fan and An Fang-mei, "Hsin-ling ti erh-chung tsou" ("Duet of the Mind"), *Chung-kuo shih-pao (China Times)*, Taipei, June 1–3, 1975.

Appendix III

1. The organic structure of poetry, according to Wen, is "to tailor one's dress according to one's size." When the framework is constructed and implemented, the "more powerful the writer, the more willing he is to dance in his shackles. . . . Form to a non-poet is an expressive barrier; for a true poet, a weapon." See Wen I-to , "Shih te ke-lu" ("Meters in Poetry") in *Wen I-to ch'uan-chi (The Complete Works of Wen I-to)*, ed. Chu Tzu-ch'ing, III (Shanghai, 1948), p. 247.

2. Fu noted the diminishing hieroglyphic significance of the Chinese language, and emphasized the connotative imagery of words rather than the pictorial imagery of characters. He further observed that despite the few strokes in the Chinese character *jen*, or "man," it nevertheless should be viewed as the image of "a round-headed, square-toed being." See Fu Tung-hua, *Shih-k'o yuan-li ABC (The ABC of Poetic Theory)* (rpt., Hong Kong, 1959), pp. 71–72.

3. Ho Ch'i-fang, *Kuan-yu hsieh-shih ho tu-shih (About Writing and Reading Poetry)* (Peking, 1957), p. 71.

4. Wang Li, "Chung-kuo ke-lu shih ti ch'uan-t'ung ho hsien-tai ke-lu shih ti wen-t'i" ("The Tradition of Chinese Regulated Verse and the Problem in Modern Regulated Verse"), *Wen-hsueh p'ing-lun*, "Literary Criticism" 4 (1961), p. 4.

5. Lu Chih-wei, "Lun chieh-tsou" ("On Rhythm"), *Wen-hsueh tsa-chih*, 1, No. 3 (n.d.), p. 12.

6. *Ibid.*, p. 18.

7. *Ibid.*, p. 18.

8. Wang Li, *Han-yu shih-lü hsueh (Versification in the Chinese Language)* (Shanghai, 1962). In first edition (1950), the fifth and final chapter was devoted to the discussion of modern Chinese versification. For unknown reasons, this chapter has been deleted in all later editions.

Selected Bibliography

PRIMARY SOURCES

Books written, translated, and edited by Feng Chih between 1927 and 1978.

Tso-jih chih ko. Kweilin: *Pei-hsin*, 1927.

Kei i-ko ch'ing-nien shih-jen ti shih-feng hsin. Translated Kunming, 1938; Hong Kong: *Chien-wen* (reprint), 1959.

Shih-ssu-hang chi. Kweilin: Ming-jih-she, 1942; Shanghai: Wen-hua sheng-huo, 1949.

Wu Tzu-hsu. Shanghai: Wen-hua sheng-huo, 1946.

Shan shui. Shanghai: Wen-hua sheng-huo, 1947.

Tung-ou tsa-chi. Peking: Jen-min wen-hsueh, 1951.

Tu Fu chuan. Peking: Jen-min wen-hsueh. 1952.

Chang Ming-shan ho fan wei-p'an. Peking: Kung-jen ch'u-pan-she, 1954.

Feng Chih shih wen hsuan-chi. Peking: Jen-min wen-hsueh, 1955.

Hai-nieh shih-hsuan., trans. Peking: Jen-min wen-hsueh, 1956.

Hsi-chiao chi. Peking Jen-min wen-hsueh, 1957.

Shih-nien shih-ch'ao. Peking: Jen-min wen hsueh, 1959.

Tu Fu shih-hsuan., ed. Peking: Jen-min wen-hsueh, 1962.

Shih yu i-ch'an. Peking: Tso-chia, 1963.

Te-kuo, i ko tung-t'ien ti t'ung-hua., trans., Peking: Jen-min wen hsueh, 1978.

SECONDARY SOURCES

1. This list contains selected articles, criticisms and books written in English on Chinese, English and American literature.

ABRAMS, M. H. *The Mirror and the Lamp*. Oxford: Oxford University Press, 1953. A sophisticated study of the Romantic theory and the critical tradition in the West.

ACTON, HAROLD. *Memoirs of an Aesthete*. London: Methuen, 1948. Contains accounts of Peking literary circles in the thirties.

———. and CH'EN SHIH-HSIANG, trans. and ed. *Modern Chinese Poetry*. London: Duckworth, 1936. One of the earliest translated poetry anthologies of modern Chinese poetry.

ALLEY, REWI, trans., FENG CHIH, comp. *Tu Fu: Selected Poems*. Peking:

Foreign Language Press, 1962. Translations of Tu Fu's poems. Good selections.

BAYS, GWENDOLYN. *The Orphic Vision.* Lincoln: University of Nebraska Press, 1964. A study of Orphism in the European tradition.

BIRCH, CYRIL, ed. *Chinese Communist Literature.* New York: Praeger, 1963. Series of articles on the literary activities of mainland China before the Hundred Flowers Movement. Good analytical and informative essays.

BOORMAN, HOWARD L., ed. *Biographical Dictionary of Republican China.* 4 vols. New York: Columbia University Press, 1967-70. An excellent source book for biographical information on modern Chinese intellectuals. Detailed and precise.

BURKE, KENNETH. "Three Definitions." *The Kenyon Review,* 8 (1951), pp. 173-92. In defining the lyric, Burke analyzes a conventional definition of the lyric and considers its implications in a series of fragmentary comments exploring the problem of definition itself.

CH'EN SHIH-HSIANG. "Metaphor and the Conscious in Chinese Poetry under Communism." *The China Quarterly,* 13 (1963), pp. 36–59. Feng Chih's poems are used to illustrate the mentality of the communist intellectuals.

Chinese Communist Who's Who. Ed. Institute of International Relations, The Republic of China, Taipei, 1970. Contains brief account of Feng Chih's political life after the Liberation.

CHOW, TSE-TSUNG. *The May Fourth Movement: Intellectual Revolution in Modern China.* Cambridge: Harvard University Press, 1960. A comprehensive pioneer study of one of the most significant intellectual movements in modern China.

——. *Research Guide to the May Fourth Movement.* Cambridge: Harvard University Press, 1960. A reference guide for the study of this movement.

DOOLIN, J. DENNIS, and CHARLES P. RIDLEY. *A Chinese-English Dictionary of Chinese Communist Terminology.* Stanford: LEE, Hoover Institute Press, 1973.

EDEL, LEON. *The Modern Psychological Novel.* New York: Universal Library, 1964. A study of the philosophic origin and the literary development of the psychological novel.

EMPSON, WILLIAM. *Some Versions of Pastoral.* New York: New Directions, 1960. Has a chapter on the relation between pastoral and proletarian literature. The author sees the pastoral convention as any work "about the people but not by or for" them.

FANG, ACHILLES. "From Imagism to Whitmanism in Recent Chinese Poetry: A Search for a Poetics That Failed," *Indiana University Conference on Oriental-Western Literary Relations.* Ed. Horst Frenz and G. L. Anderson. Chapel Hill: University of North Carolina Press,

1955, pp. 177-89. An account of the Western literary impact on modern Chinese poetics. Informative, but scope is limited.

FOKKEMA, D. W. *Literary Doctrine in China and Soviet Influence 1956–1960*. Hague: Mouton & Co., 1965. A major study of the impact of Soviet literature on communist literature in China.

FREEDMAN, RALPH. *The Lyrical Novel*. Princeton: Princeton University Press, 1963. A study of the novel as "a disguised lyric," and of its forms and tradition in Western literature.

FRYE, NORTHROP. *Anatomy of Criticism*. Princeton: Princeton University Press, 1957. An attempt to give a synoptic view of the scope, theory, principles and techniques of Western literary criticism.

GOLDMAN, MERLE. *Literary Dissent in Communist China*. Cambridge: Harvard University Press, 1967. A comprehensive work for the study of modern communist literature in China. Good insight and order.

GROSS, HARVEY, ed. *The Structure of Verse*. New York: Fawcett, 1966. Contains essays on prosody by leading Western critics. Good reference work.

HERNADI, PAUL. *Beyond Genre*. Ithaca: Cornell University Press, 1972. Advanced studies of concepts and theories of literature.

HSIA, TSI-AN. *The Gate of Darkness: Studies on the Leftist Literary Movement in China*. Seattle and London: University of Washington, 1968. Discusses the literary qualities of communist writers. Anticommunist oriented.

HSU, KAI-YU. ed. and trans. *Twentieth Century Chinese Poetry: An Anthology*. New York: Doubleday, 1963. A comprehensive presentation of modern Chinese poets. Good selections and translations.

———. *The Chinese Literary Scene*. New York: Vintage, 1975. A most up-to-date source of information on writers in the mainland after 1949.

KERMODE, FRANK. *Romantic Image*. New York: Vintage, 1957. An insightful study of Western Romanticism.

LEE, LEO OU-FAN. *The Romantic Generation of Modern Chinese Writers*. Cambridge: Harvard University Press, 1973. Main focus on the *Creation* group.

LIN, JULIA C. *Modern Chinese Poetry: An Introduction*. Seattle and London: University of Washington Press, 1972. Comprehensive, but sometimes lacks depth.

LIU, JAMES J. Y. *The Art of Chinese Poetry*. Chicago: University of Chicago Press, 1962. A brilliant study of the various aspects of Chinese poetry. Particularly strong in discussing the Chinese language as a medium of poetic expression.

LUKACS, GEORG. *Studies in European Realism*. New York: Grosset & Dunlap, 1964. A Marxist critical approach to the European fiction.

MCDOUGALL, BONNIE S. *The Introduction of Western Literary Theories into Modern China 1919-1925*. Tokyo: The Center for East Asian Cul-

tural Studies, 1971. A comparative study of East-West literary relations.

————, ed. and trans. *Paths in Dreams: Selected Prose and Poetry of Ho
Chi-fang*. Queensland: University of Queensland Press, 1976. De-
lightful translations of Ho's works.

PREMINGER, ALEX, et al., ed. *Princeton Encyclopedia of Poetry and Poetics*. Princeton: Princeton University Press, 1965. Good reference
work with keen critical insight.

RILKE, RAINER MARIA. *Duino Elegies*. Trans. J. B. Leishman and Stephen
Spender. New York: Norton, 1967.

————. *Letters to a Young Poet*. Trans. M. D. Herter Norton. New York:
Norton, 1962.

————. *Sonnets to Orpheus*. Trans. C. F. MacIntyre. Berkeley: University
of California Press, 1940.

SANDERS, TAO TAO, trans. *Red Candle: Selected Poems by Wen I-to*. London: Jonathan Cape, 1972.

SEWALL, ELIZABETH. *The Orphic Voice*. New York: Harper, 1960. One of
the best studies of Orphism in Western literature.

SCHOLES, ROBERT, and ROBERT KELLOG. *The Nature of Narrative*. New
York: Oxford University Press, 1966. A historical and analytical study
of the narrative tradition.

STOLZOVA, M. "The Foundations of Modern Chinese Poetics." *Archiv
Orientalni*, 36 (1968), pp. 585–608. Information on the beginning stage
of modern vernacular poetry.

STRAUSS, WALTER A. *Descent and Return*. Cambridge: Harvard University
Press, 1971. Traces Orpheus' metamorphosis from Novalis and Nerval
through Mallarmé and Rilke to the contemporary period.

WHEELWRIGHT, PHILIP. *Metaphor and Reality*. Bloomington: Indiana
University Press, 1962. In-depth study of metaphors as an expression
of language.

Who's Who in Communist China, rev. ed. Hong Kong: Union Research
Institute, 1969.

WILLIAMS, RAYMOND. *The Country and the City*. New York: Oxford University Press, 1973.

WILLIAMS, WILLIAM CARLOS. *Paterson*. New York: New Directions, 1963.
Hailed as a modern American epic.

YASUDA, KENNETH. *The Japanese Haiku*. Rutland: Tuttle, 1957. A
thoughtful and comprehensive study of haiku, the major lyrics in
Japan.

2. This list includes selected articles and books written in Chinese on modern Chinese literature.

AI CH'ING. "Liao-chieh tso-chia, tsun-chung tso-chia," *Chieh-fang jih-pao*

(March 11, 1942), p. 4. A controversial article which discusses whether a writer should be respected and understood by his audience.

Ao Ao. "Shih-jen yu k'uei-lei." *Ch'i-ling nien-tai yueh-pao* (May, 1971), pp. 22–24. On Feng Chih's poetic voice as an individual and a speaker for the masses.

CHAO CHIA-PI, ed. *Chung-kuo hsin wen-hsueh ta-hsi*. 10 vols. Shanghai, 1936.

CHAO TS'UNG. *Wu-ssu wen-t'an tien-ti*. Hong Kong, 1964. Casual talks on May-Fourth writers. Interesting and informative.

CHENG CHEN-TO. *Chung-kuo wen-hsueh yen-chiu*. Hong Kong, 1965. Good discussion on modern Chinese literature.

CHENG HSUEH-CHIA. *Yu wen-hsueh ke-ming tao ke wen-hsueh ti ming*. Hong Kong, 1953. Contains some information on the political role of communist literature.

CH'IEN CHI-PO. *Hsien-tai chung-kuo wen-hsueh shih*. Shanghai, 1933. One of the earliest summaries of the history of modern Chinese literature.

CHU KUANG-CH'IEN. "Hsien-tai chung-kuo wen-hsueh." *Wen-hsueh tsa-chih*, 2, No. 8 (1948), pp. 13–17. Feng Chih was discussed extensively as a contemplative poet.

———. "Hsin-shih ti k'e-lu." *Wen-hsueh p'ing-lun*, 4 (1961), p. 16. On the evolution of new forms in poetry.

———. *Wen-i hsin-li-hsueh*. Hong Kong, 1970. Comprehensive work on aesthetics; both Chinese and Western concepts are discussed and compared.

CHU TZU-CH'ING. *Hsin-shih tsa-hua*. Shanghai, 1947. Discusses various trends of new poetry in modern China.

———. *Chu Tzu-ch'ing ch'uan-chi*. 4 vols. Hong Kong, 1972.

CH'U I. "Hsin-shih ti tsung-chi yu ch'i ch'u-lu" *Wen-hsueh*, 8 No. 1, p. 21. A nonscholarly article on the modernist movement in Chinese poetry.

Chung-kuo hsien-tai wen-hsueh shih ts'an-k'ao tzu-liao. 4 vols. Peking, 1959. An excellent reference containing major articles on the proletarian literature movement.

FU TUNG-HUA. *Shih-ko yuan-li ABC*. Hong Kong, 1959. Basic and readable.

———, and CHENG CHEN-TO, ed. *Wen-hsueh pai-t'i*. Shanghai, 1935. A Chinese encyclopedia of literary theories and genres. Both Chinese and Western literatures are listed.

FUNG, M. M. Y., et al. *Hsien-tai chung-kuo shih-hsuan 1919–1949*. Hong Kong, 1974. A good anthology with short biography of each poet.

HO CH'I-FANG. *Kuan-yu hsieh-shih ho tu-shih*. Peking, 1957.

———. *Shih-ko hsin-shang*. Peking, 1962.

———. *Wen-hsueh i-shu ti ch'ung-t'ien*. Peking, 1964.

HU SHIH. *Hu Shih wen-ts'un*. 4 vols. Shanghai, 1921.

HUO I-HSIEN. *Tsui-chin erh-shih nien chung-kuo wen-hsueh shih-kang.* Canton, 1936. One of the early histories of modern Chinese literature.

KO LIANG-HSIANG. *Chung-kuo shih-lun.* Taipei, 1960. Readable.

KUO MO-JO. *Kuo Mo-jo shu-hsin chi.* Shanghai, 1937. Good documents on correspondence between Kuo and his friends.

———. *Mo-jo wen-chi.* 17 vols. Peking, 1957.

LI CHIN-FA. *P'iao-ling hsien-pi.* Taipei, 1964; Contains good autobiographical information on the first Chinese "symbolist" poet.

LI HO-LIN. *Chin erh-shih nien chung-kuo wen-i ssu-ch'ao lun.* Chungking, 1946. On the development of literary trends. Discursive and incomplete.

LI HUI-YING. *Chung-kuo hsien-tai wen-hsueh shih.* Hong Kong, 1970. Handy and useful, but sometimes superficial.

LI KUANG-T'IEN. *Shih ti i-shu.* Shanghai, 1943. An impressive work on the art of modern Chinese poetry. Feng Chih's sonnets and other poems were discussed extensively in a chapter.

LI OU-FAN. "Wu-ssu yun-tung yu lang-man chu-i," *Ta-hsueh tsa-chih,* 53 (1972), p. 14. On Chinese Romanticism in the modern era.

———, and AN FANG-MEI. "Hsin-ling ti erh-chung-tsou." *Chung-kuo shih-pao* (Taipei, June 1–3, 1975). On the gothic elements of Chinese Romanticism.

LIANG SHIH-CH'IU. *Wen-hsueh yin-yuan.* Taipei, 1964. Contains information on Romanticism and the Creascent School.

LIN MANG. *Chung-kuo hsin wen-hsueh erh-shih nien 1919–1939.* Hong Kong, 1957. Disappointing.

LO NIEN-SHENG. "Shih ti chieh-tsou." *Wen-i p'ing-lun,* 3 (1959), pp. 18–24. On poetic rhythm and the possibility of the new ballads.

LU CHIH-WEI. "Lun chieh-tsou." *Wen-hsueh tsa-chih,* 1, No. 3 (n.d.), pp. 1–20. A daring proposal of adopting the English iambic pentameter as an ideal rhythm for modern Chinese poetry. Interesting but lacks depth.

MAO TSE-TUNG. *Mao Tse-tung lun wei-i.* Peking, 1967.

PIEN CHIH-LIN. *Yu-mu chih.* Shanghai, 1935.

SHANG-KUAN YU and KO HSIEN-NING, ed. *Wu-shih nien lai ti chung-kuo shih-ko.* Taipei, 1965. Good introduction, but maintains a staunch anticommunist overtone; many leftist poets including Feng Chih are omitted.

TAI WANG-SHU. *Tai Wang-shu shih-hsuan.* Peking, 1957.

TSANG K'E-CHIA, ed. *Chung-kuo hsin shih-hsuan 1919-1949.* Peking, 1956. Reflects the contribution of leftist poets. Useful.

TUNG CH'U-P'ING. "Ts'ung Wen I-to ti 'szu-shui' t'an tao hsin k'e-lu shih wen-t'i." *Wen-i p'ing-lun,* 4 (1961), pp. 74–84. Exploring the possibility of regulated verse pattern in modern Chinese poetry.

WANG LI. "Chung-kuo k'e-lu shih ti ch'uan-t'ung ho hsien-tai k'e-lu shih ti wen-t'i." *Wen-hsueh p'ing-lun*, 4(1961), p. 4. On metrical patterns of classical and modern poetry.

——. *Han-yu shih-lu hsueh*. Shanghai, 1962. Excellent research on Chinese prosody. Indispensable for students of poetry.

WANG YAO. *Chung-kuo shih-ko fa-chan chiang-hua*. Peking, 1956. On the development of Chinese poetry. An attempt to bridge the classical and modern traditions.

——. *Chung-kuo hsin-wen-hsueh shih-kao*. Rpt. Hong Kong, 1972. Good reference for the development of proletarian literature in China.

WEN I-TO. *Wen i-to ch'uan-chi*. Ed. Chu Tzu-ch'ing. 4 vols. Shanghai, 1948. Contains Wen's poetic theories.

WU TSU-WEN, tr. and ed. *Ta-lu ti wen-t'an yu wen-jen*. Hong Kong, 1964. Contains series of articles on movements and writers in China. Useful.

Index